JAI ALAI

JAI ALAI

Paula E. Morton

A Cultural History of the Fastest Game in the World

UNIVERSITY OF NEW MEXICO PRESS ● ALBUQUERQUE

© 2019 by the University of New Mexico Press
All rights reserved. Published 2019
Printed in the United States of America

Library of Congress Cataloging-in-Publication Data
Names: Morton, Paula E., author.
Title: Jai alai: a cultural history of the fastest game in the world /
  Paula E. Morton.
Description: Albuquerque: University of New Mexico Press, 2019. |
  Includes bibliographical references and index. |
Identifiers: LCCN 2018032366 (print) | LCCN 2018045458 (e-book) |
  ISBN 9780826355508 (e-book) | ISBN 9780826355492
  (pbk.: alk. paper)
Subjects: LCSH: Jai alai—History. | Jai alai players.
Classification: LCC GV1017.P4 (e-book) |
  LCC GV1017.P4 M67 2019 (print) | DDC 796.36/4—dc23
LC record available at https://lccn.loc.gov/2018032366

Cover illustration courtesy of Fotosearch.com
Designed by Felicia Cedillos
Composed in Berling Lt Std 9.75/14

For the players

A young priest was asked by his Bishop, a little maliciously perhaps, who he would rather have been, Bossuet the preacher or Perkain the *pilotari*. The answer came without a moment's hesitation: "Perkain!"

—RODNEY GALLOP, BOOK OF THE BASQUES

The pelota went screaming down the sidewall and seemingly out of reach when Adolfo Elizegi, the fiery backcourter, fuming and down on points, dove headfirst into the fronton's cold granite floor, scooped the goatskin ball deep in the belly of his cesta and twisting in one fast, desperate motion, fired the rock-hard sphere against the front wall with a sound of shattered glass. Winner!

—GEOFFREY GRAY, "IN BASQUE COUNTRY, COMING HOME TO JAI ALAI"

Contents

Preface xi

1. "It Is a Grand Sport" 1
2. In the Beginning 19
3. The "Fastest Game in the World" 41
4. Jai Alai in Cuba 59
5. The Question of Gambling 77
6. The Rise of Jai Alai 95
7. Troubled Jai Alai 119
Epilogue 137

Glossary 141
Notes 143
Selected Bibliography 151
Index 155

Preface

> The globalization of sports is part of a much larger—and much more controversial—globalization process. . . . As a result of modern technology, people, money, images, and ideas are able to traverse the globe with tremendous speed. The development of modern sports was influenced by the interwoven economic, political, social, and cultural patterns of globalization. These patterns both enable and constrain people's actions, which means there are winners and losers in the diffusion of modern sports from Europe and North America to the rest of the world.
>
> —ALLEN GUTTMANN, JOSEPH ANTHONY MCGUIRE, WILLIAM N. THOMPSON, DAVID CHARLES ROWE, *SPORTS*

I first saw jai alai played at Casino Miami Jai Alai in Miami, Florida, in 2013. On a weekend excursion I drove some four hours from my home in St. Augustine to South Florida. I was curious. The most I knew about jai alai is that it originated in the small Basque region of Spain and France and was a speedy handball-like game played with a hard rubber ball hurled from a long, curved basket. What kind of sport merited the "Fastest Moving Ball Sport" in the Guinness World Records? Who were the players? Who were the fans? Who are the

Basques? How did jai alai evolve from a regional sport, *cesta punta*, as it is known by the Basques, into jai alai, an international sport? Why didn't jai alai catch on as a major American sport?

This is a history of jai alai that examines jai alai's rise, fall, and possible rise again. The book introduces the sport of jai alai, known for the speed of its game and the skill of its athletes. The story is about a sport created by and associated with the Basques—a sport that traveled with the Basques from Spain to Latin America, the Caribbean, Asia, and, eventually, the United States—a sport that accommodated itself to a variety of different cultures. What lay behind the changes in practice and purpose from one region to another in jai alai, what were the causes, and what were the effects?

But the book is more than a history of a fast and exciting sport. This is the story of the influence of globalization on a traditional sport, its adaptation, its rise to become a popular international sport, and its decline. It is the story of a traditional sport enhanced by globalization and then eclipsed by globalization.

To tell this story of jai alai, I consulted an intriguing array of books and articles, news clips and videos. I made on-site visits to jai alai games and conducted personal interviews. Though my sources are listed throughout the book and in the bibliography, I am indebted to the individuals who shared their knowledge and inspiration.

To the archivists and librarians, especially James Cusick, Melissa Espino, James Liversidge, Paul Losch, and Taryn Marks at the University of Florida Libraries; Dawn Hugh at the History Miami Museum; Miriam Spalding at the State Library of Florida; Kathleen Camino, Daniel Montero, and Shannon Sisco at the Center for Basque Studies, University of Nevada, Reno; the Basque Studies Program, Boise State University; Amanda Bielmann at the Basque Museum and Cultural Center; Michael Maher at the Nevada Historical Society; Jason Stratman at the Missouri History Museum; Annie Sherman at Newport Life Magazine; and Karlene Adams at St. Johns County Public Library.

To the historians and anthropologists, especially John Bieter, Joseba Etxebeste, Paul George, David Lachiondo, Viola Miglio, Gary Mormino, Daniel Nathan, Marijke Stoll, William Thompson, Carmelo Urza, and Joseba Zulaika.

To the jai alai players, especially Juan Arrasate, Robert Barrios, Ben Bueno, Francisco Churruca, Joey Cornblit, Matt DiDomizio, Pierre Echeverry, José Eizaguirre, Inaki Goikoetxea, José Goitia, Bonifacio Guenetxea, and Leon Shepard. And to those who were part of the jai alai industry, specifically Richard Berenson, Marty Fleischman, and Bob Heussler.

Thank you, John Byram, former director of the University of New Mexico Press, for suggesting the topic of jai alai, and, as always, for giving me encouragement and excellent guidance. Thank you, Elise McHugh, editor at the University of New Mexico Press, for your support and worthy contributions.

Special thanks go to my husband, Barry.

1
"IT IS A GRAND SPORT"

"**S**ay, Hi-Lie!" It was a Friday evening, prime-time television viewing between 8:00 and 11:00 p.m., depending on the time zone. The audience gathered around the television set to watch "Kill Shot," the ninth episode of the fourth season of the gritty crime drama series *Miami Vice*—then one of the hippest shows on television—featuring an entire storyline around the traditional Basque ball game of jai alai. And so, October 10, 1986, was the first time millions of people across the United States saw the sights and heard the sounds of this strange ball game.

Filmed in and around sunny, exotic Miami, the show meshed the naturally beautiful environment and exceptional multicultural dreams with the criminal underworld activities of South Florida in the 1980s. Historian Paul George describes Miami in the '80s as prosperous and vibrant, yet "drugs, along with its propensity for political intrigue, has given Miami an image of a subtropical Casablanca." *Miami Vice*'s mix of "pop-music-as-cultural-touchstone," trendsetting stars and cars, and melodramatic storytelling played into that image.

Jai alai actually had been featured on the show long before the fourth season. *Miami Vice* opened each week with fast-paced snippets of exciting and colorful Miami accompanied by the pulsating theme music composed by Jan Hammer. A skyline of pastel urban architecture bordered the blue Biscayne Bay. There were snapshots of hibiscus blossoms, palm trees, brightly colored parrots, and pink flamingos. There were horse races, car chases, and long, sleek and fast cigarette boats named after the 1930s tobacco bootlegging crafts. And then in a flash across the screen appeared Miami Jai Alai player Hector Florio in a protective helmet hurling a small ball from a large curved wicker basket. Jai alai was an iconic and exotic Florida experience.

Even under those circumstances, it is a good bet that most loyal *Miami Vice* viewers had never heard of jai alai, even though the sport had been present in the Western Hemisphere for nearly one hundred years. Until the beginning of the twentieth century, jai alai was mainly a traditional handball game that originated in the small Basque Country of Spain and France and migrated with the Spanish to Latin America. Even today the majority of the players are Basque.

The surprisingly simple goal of cesta punta, as jai alai is known in its native Basque region of north-central Spain and southwestern France, is for a player to throw a ball against a wall and make an opponent miss the return. Force *a huts*, "void" or "error" in the words of the Basque, and score. Jai alai is played on a three-walled court called the *cancha* with a front wall, left sidewall, and back wall. The front wall, the *frontis*, is constructed of solid granite blocks, often twelve inches thick, able to withstand the velocity of the ball. The court is open to spectators, who are protected from a speeding out-of-bounds ball by a wire net screen. The player catches and

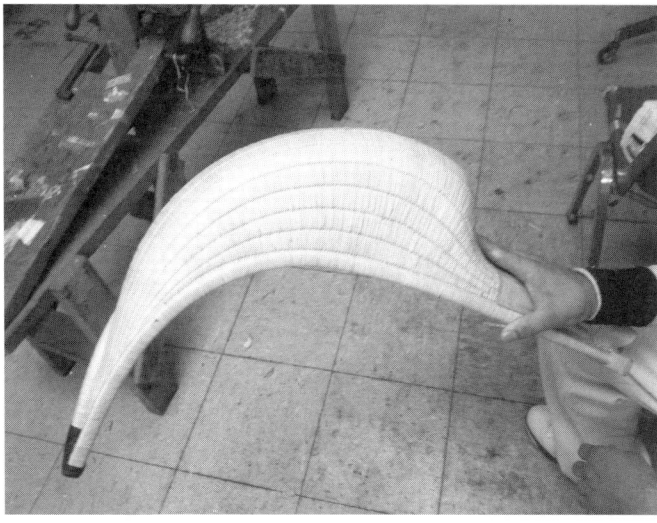

Figure 1.1. *Cesta*, the handcrafted long, curved reed basket used by the jai alai player to catch and throw a ball.

throws with the *cesta*, a custom-made long, narrow scooped out wicker basket strapped to his right hand. The cesta serves as a powerful extension of a player's right arm.

The ball, called a *pelota*, is handmade of two layers of goat skin stitched around a core of rock-hard rubber, slightly smaller than a baseball and bigger than a golf ball. It is a lethal mass thrown at high speeds from the cesta.

The server bounces the ball behind the serving line and with his cesta whips the ball against the front wall, placing the ball so it returns within the serving zone. His opponent catches the ball in mid-air or on the first bounce and sweeps the ball back to the front wall in a single continuous motion. Or the ball spins against the sidewall at an angle, forcing the opponent to climb the wall and catch the ball on the tip of his cesta. Or he does not have enough space to maneuver his cesta and misses.

"It is a grand sport," said author and jai alai aficionado Ernest Hemingway.

Yet jai alai has sputtered as an American national pastime. In 1904 the promoters of jai alai formally premiered the sport in St. Louis, Missouri, at the Louisiana Purchase Centennial Exposition, centrally located in the heartland of America: "Most Interesting, Scientific, Exciting . . . The Greatest Ball Game in the World . . . Players Secured Direct from Spain." The venture folded, the unfamiliar game failing to captivate its spectators.

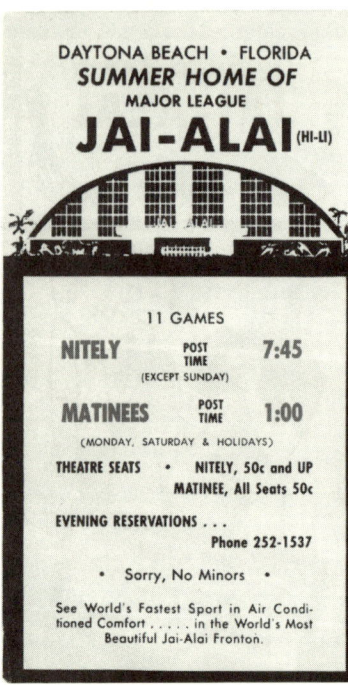

Figure 1.2. Jai alai schedule, *Daytona Beach Jai-Alai (HI-LI) Primer*, 1968.

HOW JAI-ALAI IS PLAYED

Jai-Alai is an easy game to understand. Briefly, it is played this way:

There are two different sets of games—doubles and singles.

The game starts with team 1 meeting team 2. Team 1 serves the ball against the front wall, and the ball must return between lines 4 and 7. It is then in play, with each team taking turns to return the ball against the front wall. Ball must be caught on fly or no more than one bounce, play continues until the ball is missed or a player fouls out.

The ball must be kept within the green areas of the walls. If it strikes the red, or touches the wood floor next to screen, the point is lost.

Team winning the point stays on the floor, meeting next team on the bench. Losing team returns to bench at end of line. Play continues until game point is reached.

Number of points needed to win game is one less than number of teams playing, except for American Elimination games (details on page 6). Six teams, 5 points; seven teams, 6 points, etc. Second and third places go to teams with next highest point totals. There is a playoff in case of ties. See program for details.

In singles, play is same as in doubles, but it requires more skill and endurance since one player must cover the entire court.

Figure 1.3. "How Jai-Alai Is Played," *Daytona Beach Jai-Alai (HI-LI) Primer*, 1968.

EXPLANATION JAI-ALAI

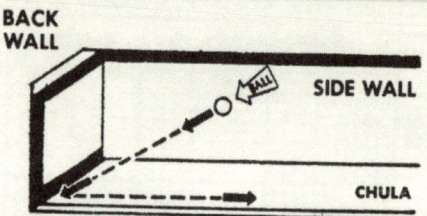

CHULA—Ball hits the base angle between the lower back wall and the floor, coming out without a bounce.

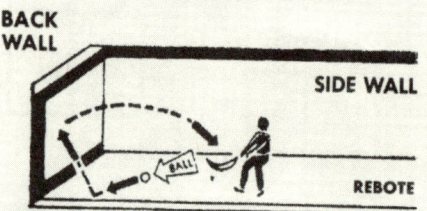

REBOTE—A return of the ball from the back wall. Made with the forehand or backhand.

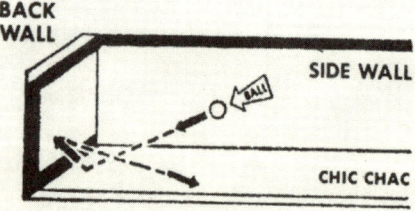

CHIC CHAC—1. Floor. —2. Back wall. —3. Floor.

Figure 1.4. "Explanation of Various Jai-Alai Shots," *Daytona Beach Jai-Alai (HI-LI) Primer*, 1968.

OF VARIOUS SHOTS—

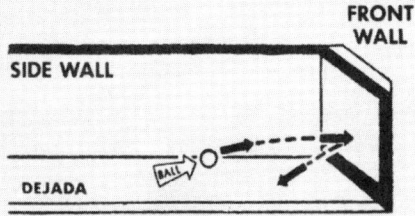

DEJADA—Short lob or easy placement; ball hits front wall just above the foul line and drops with a small bounce.

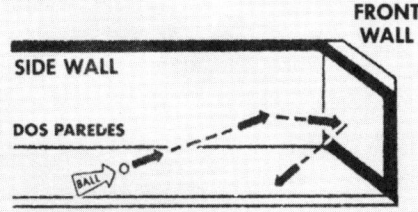

DOS PAREDES—A thrown ball that hits the side wall, the front wall then the playing court before going into screen.

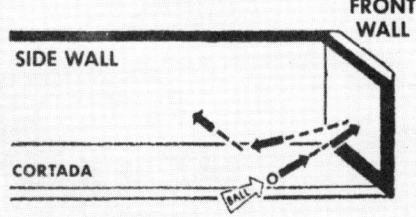

CORTADA—A ball that is thrown from outside of court with forehand, hits low on the front wall, then the floor.

Figure 1.5. "Explanation of Various Jai-Alai Shots," *Daytona Beach Jai-Alai (HI-LI) Primer*, 1968.

Eventually, the biggest concentration of fans in the United States evolved in Florida. By the beginning of the 1900s, the Spanish colonists had popularized jai alai in Havana, Cuba, little more than a hundred miles across the Straits of Florida from Key West. People, trade, ideas, and social activities flowed between the two countries, and then jai alai reached Miami. But it was not until 1935 when Florida legalized pari-mutuel betting on jai alai games that the sport expanded. Then jai alai attracted a mix of sports bettors. Some wagered for fun, others for high stakes, the total money pooled among the jai alai owners and the gamblers. The government—local, state, and federal—took its cut. Jai alai thrived. In time, ten professional frontons, buildings specifically to play jai alai, sprang up throughout Florida.

By the mid-1970s, the business of jai alai, part sport, part gambling, migrated north to three frontons in Connecticut and one in Rhode Island. Still, it remained a regional attraction dependent on the regional patchwork of federal and state gambling laws. All of which is to say that jai alai at the time of its starring role in *Miami Vice* had a lot of educating to do about the players, rules of the game, equipment, strategy, and betting.

The "Kill Shot" writers spun a prime-time soap opera tale of drug trafficking, blackmail, murder, and revenge. A high-living jai alai player known as Tico is framed by cocaine dealers for choking a prostitute to death, which leads to Tico's brother, United States customs agent Frank Arriola (portrayed by Carlos Cestenos), being blackmailed by the drug smugglers. Undercover detectives Sonny Crockett (portrayed by Don Johnson) and Rico Tubbs (portrayed by Philip Michael Thomas), battle the drug dealers "tied in with the hooker killing."

Miami Vice's "Kill Shot" was the story of jai alai at a time and in a place when thousands of fans filled the grand Miami fronton, once known as the "Yankee Stadium of Jai Alai." The crack of the hard rubber ball against the granite front wall! The speed of the ball as fast as 140 mph, 150 mph, maybe more! Players leaping, twisting, and crashing into walls! Bettors cashing a winning ticket or tearing up a losing one!

Then there was the episode's namesake "kill shot," the *remate*, the winning shot thrown so forcefully or placed so perfectly it could not be returned. It was a killer of a shot for the writers at *Miami Vice*. So it happened that champion jai alai player Tico Arriola, portrayed by Fernando Allende, took his eye off the flying ball, and it struck him on the temple and killed him. "Dead on court, struck with pelota."

Real-time Miami, real-time jai alai. Directors, actors, extras, camerapersons, stage crew, the entire production team set up to film the game scene at Miami Jai Alai on Northwest 37th Avenue, near the Miami International Airport. For three days Marty Fleischman, at the time public relations director for World Jai Alai Inc., the parent company of Miami Jai Alai, juggled filmed games with professional games at the fronton.

The audience was authentic. Local newspapers spread the word: Wanted, jai alai fans for the filming of the *Miami Vice* episode of "Kill Shot." Portray yourselves! "Everyone wanted to see Don Johnson and Philip Michael Thomas in the flesh," says Fleischman.

Thousands of recruits, the loyal regulars, filed into the stands for the shooting of the game scene. The old timers, Cuban exiles, pitted their wits against players' strategy. Groupies, women of all ages, followed their favorite charismatic players. Serious gamblers gambled. And the weekend crowd attended their entertaining night out at jai alai.

For the game shots, the Miami Jai Alai roster, traditionally male and predominately Basque, constituted the athletes. Dressed in white trousers, colored sashes, and numbered shirts, the players, called *pelotaris*, marched onto the court to the music of "March of the Toreador" and saluted the audience with their cestas strapped to their right hands. The made-for-TV authentic game began.

Close-up shots showed the actor Allende as Tico. Cesta in hand, Allende had to learn to propel the ball, sometimes 130 feet, to the front wall, and catch the rebound without the ball rolling up the curve of the cesta and dropping on the floor in front or falling behind him. But sometimes it was best that one of Miami's pro jai alai players stand in for Allende's long volleys of action during the fast-paced game.

Fleischman played himself as the sports announcer. "I only flinched once," he says, "when Tubbs attended the jai alai game to see Tico play and spoke the line, 'I never bet on anything that can talk.' Here it was, the dreaded question, is the game fixed?" Although scandals attached to match fixing by jai alai players had been relatively few in the United States, any indication that the jai alai player threw a match was a public relations nightmare for Fleischman.

A player missed what appeared to be an easy shot? Someone in the crowd, usually a frustrated bettor, was bound to shout "Fix!" That made the Basque players angry. "We play for honor, for pride," says former jai alai professional José Goitia. "Play honestly; the *plaza* (the public) is always judge" is the moral mandate on the plaque at the plaza in the Basque village of Aldudes, France. The professional player incurred an added responsibility. If he did not play well, management reduced his bonus, cut his salary, or worse, did not renew his playing contract.

All Jai-Alai Players Must Play TO WIN WHY?

THE RULE WITH TEETH

"Any player who at any time is adjudged dishonest; or thought to be intentionally playing an inferior grade of Jai-Alai; or guilty of breaking training rules; or in any way conducting himself in a manner unbecoming a gentleman, or detrimental to the best interests of Jai-Alai, must be immediately suspended and a report filed with the Florida State Racing Commission by the Players' Manager. He must further file a report with all other Frontons in the world.

"Such players are automatically SUSPENDED for life.

"Frontons maintain a world-wide investigation-service and each candidate is thoroughly screened and investigated, not only as to his ability but as to character and reputation before a contract is offered."

Figure 1.6. "All Jai-Alai Players Must Play *to Win* Why?," *Daytona Beach Jai-Alai (HI-LI) Primer*, 1968.

Was "Kill Shot" a shot in the arm for the sport of jai alai or a shot in the foot? An entire episode associating jai alai with drugs and murder, and organized crime? Was this the sports story Miami Jai Alai wanted to present?

In particular, organized crime was a sensitive issue for jai alai in the United States. Gambling exacerbated the questionable side of sports wagering that included allegations of rigged games, political corruption and money laundering. Jai alai involved the gaming business of pari-mutuel wagering in venues much less familiar than those similarly devoted to horse racing. An opportunity, disgruntled bettors and gambling opponents said, for organized crime to share a piece of the betting action.

And people remembered. On May 27, 1981, Roger Wheeler, the owner of World Jai Alai, was killed in a gangland-style shooting. John Martorano shot Wheeler point-blank in the head in the parking lot of Southern Hills Country Club in Tulsa, Oklahoma. State and federal investigators debated the definitive motive, but no doubt, Martorano was associated with the notorious "Winter Hill Gang" run by James (Whitey) Bulger. Not surprising, the people at World Jai Alai in Miami were concerned about a backlash.

Reservations aside, the corporate leaders of World Jai Alai recognized that *Miami Vice* offered a golden public relations opportunity for a sport that needed national exposure to generate interest. For by the late twentieth century, "sport in America, today, as in other parts of the world, is an institution battered by media hype, photo-ops, and sound bytes [sic]," says anthropologist Kendall Blanchard. If *Miami Vice* could change television with cinematic techniques and spur the restoration of the architectural gem of South Beach, why then, it could boost jai alai.

If asked, many "Kill Shot" viewers likely said, "Give us more jai alai. It's fast. Look at the players, fearless, throwing themselves on the floor, or climbing a wall to save a point." But the response made little difference in the outcome of jai alai as a sports industry. Two years after jai alai merited the attention of a major television show, in 1988 the players in the United States organized a strike. It was a nasty strike lasting three years, the longest professional sports-related strike in history.

American jai alai did not fully recover. Fans went elsewhere for their sports thrills and gaming. Individual states ran lotteries, professional sports leagues expanded, Native American casinos opened, and jai alai frontons closed. The time for jai alai appeared to have passed.

●

Casino Miami Jai Alai, Miami, Florida: February 7, 2014

His name is Iñaki Osa Goikoetxea, "Goiko" to his fans, and he is a nine-time World Jai Alai champion. He was born and raised in Zumaia, a fishing town on the Bay of Biscay along the Basque coast of Spain about twenty miles from San Sabastian. His father fishes for tuna in the deep waters and is often gone from home for weeks at sea. Tuna catch and prices fluctuate, so it can be a hard life.

Traditionally the Basques farmed and raised sheep and cattle in the mountain valleys and on the hillsides, while along the coast the Basques built ships, sailed, and fished. Since at least the eleventh century they commercially hunted whales. They crewed for Christopher Columbus on his first voyage to the Americas in 1492, and then on subsequent voyages. In 1521 when explorer Ferdinand Magellan was killed by the natives in the Philippines, Basque navigator Juan Sebastian de Elcano completed the trip on the *Victoria* to circumnavigate the globe.

But Goiko did not want to be involved with the maritime tradition. He wanted to surf, "even in the winter." When others organized Basque handball games on Saturdays and Sundays, he tested the waves on one of the town beaches, Itzurun or Santiago, waiting for the biggest swells. However, he learned to play jai alai, coached by his two older brothers who played professional jai alai in Miami.

When he was sixteen years old Goiko's father offered him a choice: "Go to school or fish with me." Instead, Goiko chose a third option, jai alai and the opportunity to make a decent living as a professional in the United States. Initially he signed a contract to play in Italy, then Newport, Rhode Island, and from there to Orlando, Florida, and then Miami. He brought his surfboard with him when he moved to Miami but encountered a shark in the Atlantic waters and said, "Maybe I won't surf so much here."

Goiko is six-three and weighs about two hundred pounds. Handsome, he promotes jai alai on a French television commercial. He is a spectacular athlete, climbing to execute an up-the-wall shot, twisting to catch off-the-back wall returns, and throwing a carom so the ball hits the left wall and then the front wall. He has been called the Michael Jordon of jai alai, but he acknowledges, "I am not famous outside the jai alai world."

On this typical Friday performance at Casino Miami Jai Alai, Goiko bounces the ball behind the serving line and in one fluid motion of the cesta hurls the ball in a harmonious swoop to the front granite wall. He competes before thirty or so spectators, a crowd by today's standard, spread out in tiers of stands built to seat fourteen thousand. A smattering of retirees, mostly from Miami's Cuban community, shout "Mucho!" (Good catch), or "You didn't get that ball?" There are no long lines at the in-house betting windows.

In the glory days of the 1950s, '60s, '70s, and '80s, Miami Jai Alai attracted thousands of fans, even men in suits and ties, women in elegant dresses. To the side of the once grand lobby is a small room called the museum, filled with faded photographs and newsclips that tell the story of forgotten jai alai champions and their fans. In the early days of his career, actor and musician Desi Arnaz, a Cuban refugee, led his band with the sounds of the rumba to entertain spectators between game performances. Champion player Estanislao Maiztegui, known as Pistón, traveled from Havana Jai Alai to play in Miami. New York Yankees baseball hero Babe Ruth swung at the ball with a cesta, and First Lady Eleanor Roosevelt accepted a trophy for most ardent fan. "So jai alai must be a great game," reported the St. Petersburg Times.

Today the crowds gravitate to the glitz of the casino in the opposite section of the building where they place their chips on the poker table and feed coins into slot machines. Occasionally, they glance at the large closed-circuit television screens, and for a nanosecond, mesmerized, they gasp as the jai alai player climbs half up the court wall, scoops up the ball and slams it pass his opponent. And then they go back to business as usual, hoping to beat the house.

Goiko is front and center about his feelings as a dedicated and proud athlete in an overlooked sport. "When I play, the best of me comes out, wanting to win. I give all I have. The audience does not affect my play because I do my best every day. For me, jai alai is everything."

Passion and rich history surround the sport of jai alai. It is one of the few spectator sports that encourages betting on players whose individual skills outshine team strategy. Most historians agree jai alai, a variant of handball, is rooted in the distinctive Basque culture. Originally, on Sundays and Fiesta Days the Basque competed in red-blooded games of dragging rocks, stone-lifting, and pelota, or handball. Contestants and spectators bet on the outcome. It was not long before the handball players strapped custom-made curved wicker scoops to their right hand and hurled the small, hard ball long and fast in spectacular volleys. The exterior walls of the church and the additional left-hand wall of the courtyard were perfect for their game. No surprise, they broke a few stained glass windows. Even today, some priests forbid playing jai alai in the church courtyards.

ARRA'S STORY

One day in 1972, when I was thirteen years old, my friend Sarria and I decided after a game of soccer on the beach to go to the fronton to play handball. Little did I know, but that decision was going to shape the rest of my life. While we were playing handball a man appeared at the fronton with eight jai alai baskets in his hands. He told us that Miami Jai Alai was opening a school in my town of Lekeitio in the Basque province Biscay. I took a basket from him and put it on my hand. The sensation I felt was incredible. When I threw the first ball I instantly fell in love with the sport. Three years later I turned professional at the age of sixteen, and one and a half years later I came to the United States to play. I was fortunate enough to play for twenty years and be a part of the glory years. Unfortunately, the sport I love so much has been on the decline and the most frustrating thing for me is that I cannot find a solution to stop it. It saddens me to think that this sport may someday not exist.

—Juan Arrasate, Professional Jai Alai Player

Figure 1.7. "My little brother Carlos and I in 1972 at the fronton in my home town Lekeitio, Spain." Jai alai player Juan Arrasate. Courtesy of Juan Arrasate.

Royalty loved the early Basque court handball games. Henry VII, the king of England from 1485–1509, contributed a gift of one hundred English pounds to the champion Basque pelota player.

Artists painted the swinging and leaping players. In 1779 Francisco Goya depicted three pairs of players and twenty-five spectators in *Juego de Pelota*, a tapestry he created for Pardo Palace in Madrid, Spain.

Writers borrowed metaphors from the game: "The truth is I reached the gate (of Hell), where about a dozen devils were playing pelota, all of them in tights and doublets, their collars trimmed with borders of Flemish lace and cuffs of the same material, exposing four fingers' width of arm so that their hands appeared longer, and in them they were holding bats of fire, and what amazed me most was that instead of balls they were using books, apparently full of wind and trash," wrote Miguel de Cervantes in *Don Quixote*.

The Basque traveled. They explored, missionized, traded, and immigrated. As they ventured far from their homeland, these adventurers exchanged, borrowed, and adapted to other cultures, but still were determined to hold onto their Basque identity. Jai alai is significant because of how the sport has accommodated itself to a variety of cultures. How is jai alai seen by different people at different times? What are the forces behind the game, from the wrapped ball with a core of rubber, a discovery of Mesoamerica, to the longer and deeper cesta created by a Basque player in Buenos Aires, Argentina, an innovation that revolutionized the game?

Today, while jai alai's impact has cooled somewhat, it continues to be a vibrant cultural touchstone. And it started with a wall and a ball.

2

IN THE BEGINNING

On November 25, 1890, the Egypt Exploration Fund sponsored British Egyptologist Perry Newberry to survey the tombs and trace wall paintings at the Egyptian burial site of Beni Hasan. In Cairo the survey party stocked provisions and embarked on the trip south along the narrow Nile River Valley, about 155 hot and dusty miles to the town of present-day el Minya. From there they continued an additional twelve miles to the limestone cliffs on the banks of the Nile River. They climbed the steep hillside rising from the river plain, paused at the top to gaze at the panoramic view of the winding river, and then turned to attend to the task at hand: the tombs of Beni Hasan, thirty-nine tombs of the eleventh and twelfth dynasty cut into thick white limestone.

These were the burial sites of provincial nobles and government officials living and working in the Middle Kingdom of Egypt (2040–1782 BC). Entering through the outer court of the tombs, the archaeologists passed through a doorway into a rock-cut chamber where they accessed a sloping shaft to the inner burial room. At best, the archaeologists might find an intact mummified body in a decorated wood coffin called the sarcophagus, with pottery, wooden figures, and funeral objects scattered around the chamber. At worst, the tomb would have already been plundered. Yet fragments of painted wall murals survived.

For posterity and passage into the afterlife the elite enlisted artisans to paint the tomb walls with scenes of everyday life and biographical inscriptions. By the dim light of torches and lampwicks floating in oil, the painters skimmed the flaky and absorbent limestone surface with a thin coat of fine plaster before applying color pigments. They painted a single scene or filled a wall from ceiling to floor. It was among these portraits of daily life—marsh birds in an acacia tree, men hunting in the desert with netting, pairs of wrestlers in various stages of sequence of action—that the artists depicted the ancient Egyptian notion of ball playing.

On the walls of the tomb of Baqet III, identified as Tomb No. 15, and Khety, Tomb No. 17, the common women ground grain and spun flaxseed into yarn to weave into cloth while young girls with braids of elaborately plaited hair danced, juggled, and played catch and throw. "The most athletic game is a form of 'piggy-back' catch, where the thrower, apparently unhindered by her calf-length sheath dress, sits on her friend's back. It seems likely that a dropped ball resulted in the thrower and her carrier changing positons," says archaeologist and Egyptologist Joyce Tyldesley.

Separated from the girls, groups of boys knocked a ball along the ground with a club or stick, suggesting a more formal game of competitive play with rules—an early form of hockey?

But at Beni Hasan there is no trace of wall and ball games in the archeological record. The Egyptians did not know about rubber. Instead, for game balls they sewed leather or linen around a solid wood or clay sphere, or stuffed an animal skin with dry papyrus reeds, barley husks, rags, or strips of palm leaf. The ball was dull and heavy. A player threw the ball against the hard stone wall: thud, and the ball fell to the ground. The player walked away. For how could he keep the ball in play when it did not bounce back through the air after hitting the wall? As wall-and-ball games go, the early Egyptian ball was a dud.

Not so centuries later in Mexico City. Here in the postrevolutionary Mexico of the 1920s, one proud Basque jai alai star, Erdoza Menor, challenged two worthy opponents to a Spanish-style variation of jai alai known as *partido*. Normally a contest of two against two, Menor challenged them to two against one, point by point, in which the first side to reach forty points would win the match. Partido is a grueling game that takes hours to play. They played the wall-and-ball game of jai alai with a fast and lively wrapped ball with a hard core of virgin rubber, a discovery fifteenth- and sixteenth-century Spanish explorers introduced to Europe from Latin and South America.

Menor was born in 1886 in a mountain village outside of Marquina, in the Basque region of Spain, popularly known as the birthplace of jai alai. By the time he was sixteen years old he was playing professional jai alai in Mexico and Cuba, earning as much as five thousand dollars a month. He was a rich man from a country miller's family.

On this night of play, Menor and his opponents ran up and down Mexico City's 235-foot-long court, longer than today's 176-foot-long court in Miami, Florida. It took a lot of strength and stamina to hurl the ball from the curved wicker cesta to the distant front wall. If they tired or lost their concentration, they faced defeat. Tonight Menor did not tire or lose concentration, but he made one mistake, one miscalculation that almost resulted in disaster.

On top of his game and the score, Menor charged and smashed the ball at close range against the granite front wall. He killed it, a fast hard kill shot, difficult to return. Once Menor released his shot, he knew he had to move quickly to get out of the way of the bounce-back. Dodge, he thought. But he was out of place, and the rebound came fast, slamming into his leg with full force. He fell to the floor, they carried him off the court, and the game was over. Or, was it? Menor returned, hobbling with a wounded leg swollen to twice its normal size.

His opponents scored three points in row. Menor paused, faced the sidewall, turned his back to the audience, swung his cesta, turned around, and resumed play. Those were the last points he allowed. He won. Thus, "El Fenomeno," the phenomenon, was born.

Menor continued playing past his peak until at age fifty-four, midway through a long match in Spain, he sprinted toward the front wall, whacked the ball, ran back to the service line, and dropped dead from a heart attack. "It was just that he couldn't live without jai alai," his son told author Katherine Hines Herrington. For Menor was a Basque, tenacious and independent, dedicated to the sport rooted in his traditional culture.

Jai alai is at home in the Basque Country, *Euskalherria*, land of the Euskara speakers. The Basques live in four provinces in north-central Spain—Navarra (*Nafarroa*), Guipúzcoa (*Gipuzkoa*), Vizcaya (*Bizkaia*), and Alava (*Araba*), and three in the southwestern corner of France—Labourd (*Lapurdi*), Basse Navarre (*Basse Navarre*), and Soule (*Xiberoa*). They live in the

Figure 2.1. Traditional Basque rural homestead in the foothills of the Western Pyrenees between Spain and France. Courtesy of José Goitia.

pine forest foothills of the western Pyrenees and on the rocky seacoast of the Bay of Biscay. The total region straddling the French and Spanish borders is about 8,218 square miles, about the size of Rhode Island. It is a small geographical homeland yet large in historical depth.

Who are the Basque people? "There are few races on the face of the earth of whose origin so little is known, and who have exercised such a fascination over ethnologists and philologists of every nationality," said author Rodney Gallop. Basques are a distinct people and want to keep it that way.

The fascination has exhibited itself in a variety of creative ways. Anthropologists once analyzed the structure of Basque skulls and compared them with those of European early humans who existed about 43,000 years ago, and then examined the skulls of Laplanders and ancestral Hungarians and Germans. The researchers could establish no definitive line of direct descendants.

Biologists have found the Basques predominantly have blood type O, rarely type B, and a high incidence of Rhesus negative blood. "Most investigators have argued that, at the very least, Basques have constituted a somewhat isolated genetic pool within Europe over a considerable period of time," concur anthropologists William Douglass and Joseba Zulaika.

There is also the archaeological record of human occupation. In three caves, Isturitz, Oxocelhaya, and Erberua, in the French Basque region, archaeologists excavated prehistoric flint stone implements from the Mousterian Era, forty to eighty thousand years ago. In the Spanish Basque-region caves, researchers discovered prehistoric cave art at Altamira and Askondo dating back an estimated eighteen to twenty-five thousand years. And the Basque people as an ethnic group with a shared cultural heritage of language, customs, and institutions? Evidence indicates they have inhabited their original homeland for at least the past five thousand years, and probably more.

The Basques made their home in their ancestral land long before the third century BC when the Carthaginian army marched through the Pyrenees mountain passes to the Iberian Peninsula, followed by the Romans, who warred against Carthage, won, and occupied the Basque territory. Rome fell and the Visigoths, a Germanic people, conquered the Basques in AD 415. By the early eighth century, the Moors from North Africa moved into the Basque lowlands, yet were thwarted from complete domination in the northern mountainous region. In these foothills of the Basque Mountains in AD 778, the Basques ambushed the rear guard of the army of Charlemagne, Charles the Great, at Roncesvalles Pass, and chased them back to France. The

Basque coup was Charlemagne's only military defeat. But it was not until the Christian forces defeated the Moors after an eight-hundred-year conflict that Spain, and then France, divided the Basque Country. "The singular remarkable fact about the Basques is that they still exist," says author Mark Kurlansky.

These are the people who may be the oldest identifiable ethnic culture in Europe. Yet they did not write about their world until 1545, when Bernard Dechepare published the first book in the Basque language, a collection of religious and erotic poems titled *Linguae Vasconum Primitiae*. Instead, it was the Romans who were the earliest chroniclers of the Basques. The invaders wrote documentaries defending Roman occupation and values. These narratives described the rugged mountain farms and fishing villages and depicted the Basques as a reserved yet festive people with an unusual language.

The Basques speak Euskara, a language unlike any of the Indo-European languages, a family of several hundred languages spoken over the greater part of Europe and Asia and as far as northern India. Although linguists find some borrowed vocabulary and grammar forms, they are unable to link the Basque language with other dialects. "By far the most telling evidence for the uniqueness of the Basques is the testimony of their language," remark Douglass and Zulaika.

"To think in Basque requires an entirely different attitude of mind from that inherent in other more familiar languages," said Gallop. The verbs and sentence structure are complex, the sounds guttural, there are no prepositions or articles, and the dialects are diverse. Too difficult a language even for the devil to learn, the legends say. After seven years of listening in on Basque conversations the devil only knew "*bai*" (yes) and "*ez*" (no).

"I would like to invite you to pronounce the longest surname in Euzkara, Iturriberrigorrigoikoerrotakoetxea," says professional jai alai player and Basque native José Goitia. No wonder the first thing a Basque jai alai player does is adopt a short playing name. Sports fans following the "fastest game in the world" do not have time to shout a tongue twister.

Logically, Pedro Yarza declared he was "El Manco de Villabona" (the one-armed of Villabona). He was from Villabona, Spain, and had one arm. Despite losing his right arm in a childhood accident, Yarza played extraordinarily well with his left, an anomaly for the right-handed game of jai alai. Jose Antonio Illoro assumed the Basque name of his hometown, Bolibar, changed by his manager to the Spanish "Bolivar," changed by his fans to "Boli, Boli." In recent times, Iñaki Osa Goikoetxea simply shortened his family name to "Goiko," while Bonifacio Guexetxea became "Boni."

What is undeniable is that the language Euskara is distinctively Basque, an integral part of the Basque identity. For the Basques are Euskaldunak, "holders of the language," or speakers of Euskara. At home or far from home, the Basque people figured out what their identity was about before they lost it. They claim for themselves the Basque language, a self-determined system of laws called *fueros*, the independence group Euskadi Ta Askatasuna (ETA), and family roots in the house of their clan, *etxea*. They share with the world the espadrille shoe, a black piebald pig, the beret, and jai alai.

In the Basque Country men and women wear espadrilles, or *espardenyas*, traditionally a flat shoe with a canvas top and jute rope sole. At one time soldiers went to war wearing espadrilles; shepherds, farmers, and fishermen wore them. Even Don Johnson in his star role as Sonny Crockett in the

1980s television series *Miami Vice* adopted this distinctive style. There he was attending the jai alai game in the "Kill Shot" episode wearing his signature T-shirt with a sports jacket, linen pants, and sockless slip-on espadrilles. Today the wearing of the espadrille, traditional or designer style with a wedge heel, is universal, far beyond the Basque borders.

In the Basque Country, farmers and stockbreeders raise the *Euskal Txerria*, known variously as the Basque Pig, or *Porc Basque*, or *Porc Pie Noir du Pais Basque* (Black Foot Pig from the Basque Country). Raising and breeding domestic swine has been an important part of the Basque economy and the native Basque Pig, a breed of Iberic pig with black and white bicolored skin, is a favorite. The rugged yet docile Basque Pig, with strong thick legs and ample fat coverage, is adapted to the free-range tradition. In the forests and on the mountainsides, the pig shelters in wood huts and roams to feed on herbs, chestnuts, acorns, and ferns, supplemented with cereal grains by the farmer. Unlike lean swine bred to accommodate modern tastes, the Basque Pig is prized for its high animal fat specific for the production of air-dried salted Bayonne Ham stamped with the traditional Basque cross *lauburu* and sold in international markets.

On quiet village plazas old men with bushy eyebrows and the typical long, straight nose play the Basque game of cards, *mus*, and they wear the Basque beret. The traditional Basque beret, or *txapela*, is a round flat soft cap of wool or cloth closed in the center with the remaining stub of thread called the *txortena* (wick). At different times in history, the beret protected shepherds from sun and rain, identified the red-bereted Carlists in the nineteenth-century Spanish civil wars, and topped the exotic image of Hollywood star Greta Garbo. Back in 1951 in Eibar, Spain, after Barberito scored the winning point in the championship handball competition, his fans removed their berets and threw them onto the court. They consecrated Barberito with "the throwing of the *txapelas*."

Even today in the Basque Country, boys and men play the wall and ball game *pelota vasca*, simply known as pelota. They play on a simple outdoor court paved with flagstones and walls often shared with the ubiquitous stone church on one side of the plaza. Sometimes the court is a long rectangular court with smooth concrete floor and three walls, but no roof to weather the cold rain of Basque winters and no screen in front of the open right wall to protect the spectators from an errant ball. Occasionally the court is enclosed, a large commercial fronton expensive to build and maintain, with a regulation competition court and seating for spectators.

"Pelota is one of the most significant cultural manifestations for the Basques," says anthropologist Olatz González Abrisketa.

Learn, children,
To speak Basque, Play pelota,
And dance correctly
(Basque popular song)

Traditionally organized around market day or festivals, since the early games the men played various versions of Basque handball to compete and bond, while the spectators gathered to unite. Crowds flocked to the matches on the plaza, watching from stands, balconies, and even tree limbs. They sang, cheered, ate, drank, and bet. Even when Francisco Franco, dictator of Spain from 1939 until his death in 1975, forbid the Basques to speak their language or celebrate their festivals, they still played Basque Ball. "Basque pelota was one of those

Figure 2.2. *Partie de robot at St-Jean-de-Luz en 1927*. Priest playing an early variation of Basque pelota at St.-Jean-de-Luz, 1927. *La Pelote Basque*, E. Blazy, 1929.

cultural icons which served both as a form of recreation and as a cultural sacrament," says historian Carmelo Urza.

A THROW OF PELOTA

"What is a Basque?" Orson Welles once asked while standing in a jai alai fronton. "We can only say what a Basque is *not*," he answered himself.

A best-known traditional song tells children to learn three things: to speak Basque, dance well, and play pelota.

That dance and language of pelota inaugurates the *not*. *Zero* is the axiomatic number in modern mathematics and subjectivity. In the game of jai alai the goal is to force the opponent to *miss* a return, that is, to make a huts, a pivotal concept that in Basque means not only "error" but also "void" or "zero." Prisoner of the moves of the erratic ball, the eyes, imagination, strategy, and desire of the jai alai fan rebound from one player to the other, from hand to wall, from ground to air, earth to sky, until at one point a huts ("void") brings the play to a standstill. In pelota, scoring is forcing a void. A *zero* is created and order returns to the breathless intensity of an otherwise unending game.

Not only is the Basque player, as Welles would have it, *not* Spanish and *not* French and *not* an interminable list of other qualifications, but in the play of his or her most intimate identity s/he is the nothingness of a huts. No wonder that the aesthetics developed by the paradigmatic sculptors Jorge Oteiza and Eduardo Chillida was anchored on the notion of huts, a term that is present of many of their works. For traditional folk curers, producing the "emptiness" of huts was equivalent to producing a "cure." The flying queen of Basque traditional mythology, folklorists tell us, is cryptically "nourished by the *no*," a nod to current theories of feminine subjectivity as characterized by the *not-all*. The jai alai fan's endless enjoyment is simply nourished by the scoring of the huts that punctuates the game, the zero that provides rhythm and control to desire.

The zero . . . and then the infinity of the subject of play. The poet Mallarmé knew it best: "A throw of the dice will never eliminate chance"—a throw of the dice, a play of cards, a pelota serve. The capricious and undefeated goddess of infinite chance, always there for those who, even in a shipwreck, dare take risks and endure the jai alai. A puppet

in the hands of gods, the player mocks questions of why
and for what; all that matters is that one conspires against
the laws of the universe, against the *not*, with all the tricks of
games, lotteries, and rebounding balls, until one finds out that
the dice of Zeus fall ever luckily—for every throw of a pelota
serve is new, everything probability and grace.

—Joseba Zulaika, Anthropologist, Center of
Basque Studies, University of Nevada, Reno

Why did the early Basques develop their particular style of court handball as their national sport? In the eleventh and twelfth century monks and villagers in southern France, neighbors of the Basques, played *jeu de paume*, game of the palm, ancestor of modern lawn tennis. Originally on a rectangular walled court, two men faced each other on opposite sides of a sagging net and hit a ball made of wool or cotton string wound and covered with leather. They played with their bare hands, similar to an early form of pelota, *pelote* in French. The heavy ball skidded and landed flat.

In the fourteenth century and into the seventeenth century the French, particularly the elite, played jeu de paume with small, teardrop-shaped rackets. Likely, important and powerful Basque families familiarized themselves with the game. However, a large part of the Basque population were working-class people—farmers, cattlemen, fishermen, and shipbuilders—steadfast and independent. They never grew to love jeu de paume as the upper-class Basque families did; they remained committed to their pelota.

The Basque people continued to play court ball on the

common level with their bare hands. Always, they tried to figure out what would make the ball go faster and harder. In 1493 Italian explorer Christopher Columbus returned to Spain from his second voyage to the Americas and presented a gift to the Spanish royal court: a rubber ball used in the Mesoamerican ball games of the Aztec and Maya. The ball bounced. The Basques took note.

By the sixteenth century, the Basques implemented the rubber ball to play their games, reportedly the first Europeans to do so. Now the players threw the game ball fast and returned it hard, and the ball game where the players faced the front wall was a game for the fit. It required little fancy equipment or courts and demanded a lot of skill and strength, features appealing to the Basque character. The Basques speak of *indarra*, force or strength, and also *sendotasuna*, physical prowess and strength of character.

In 1836 Charles Goodyear patented vulcanized rubber applied to pencil erasers, waterproof boots, and durable rubber balls. The Basques elaborated their handball specialties with the hardness of the solid vulcanized ball, different court sizes and number of walls, and how the game was played. There was *pelota a mano* played with bare hand and the two-and-a-half-inch rubber ball. There was *pelota a pala* played with the *pala*, a flat paddle of rounded wood. The most daring was cesta punta, internationally known as jai alai, played with the narrow curved cesta, Spanish for basket, strapped to the player's right hand. Often the Basques refer to jai alai and handball in the same general term, *pelota*, the Spanish word for ball.

THE EVOLUTION OF BASQUE PELOTA GAMES: RULES, SHOW BUSINESS, AND BETTING

We Basques play ball. If you scratch the skin of a Basque, you always find a *pelotari*, a ball player. My father taught his children, all the brothers, to play with the *paleta*, a solid wooden paddle of 550 to 600 grams (approximately 1.5 pounds). I, who was the youngest and could barely carry the weight of the wood, played with him, while my two older brothers doubled up against us. The games could be won or lost, but I don't remember ever playing only for fun.

Playing Basque pelota ball is serious business, like the *mus* card game. What one team wins, the other loses. It is a game without ambiguities, of clear ties, and one that ends with a clear winner and a defeated opponent. It is not unusual that friendly games often lead to family disputes: winning is everything. It is what in Euskara, the language of the Basques, is defined as a *joko*. This type of game is a model of playful behavior in defense of the public interests of the family household, the *etxe*, the center of Basque social life, against the interests of outsiders, the *kanpokoak*, from other households.

There are other ways to play Basque pelota that are not joko, but *jolas*. Here the relation can be ambiguous, and it is not clear who wins and who loses. These types of games, like the *putxe*, also called *al punto*, *a barnes*, or *la porte*, consist of hitting the ball with the bare hand against the wall until one player falters, which forces him to take a position in the front and attempt to catch a ball on the fly played by the others who restart the game. If successful, he will change positions with the hitter. This way, little by little, and after many comings and goings from the court to the front and vice versa, a single player remains, who gains a point or "life," which will allow him to miss in the upcoming match, because the game will restart with all the players again without a definite end. The jolas is the model of play for members of the same household, or *etxekoak*.

The importance of the jolas is to enjoy the relationship between the players, while in the joko it is the outcome of the contest that counts. In this manner, the jolas is inclusive and accepts in the game all the members of the household without distinction of age or sex; while the joko tends to segregate men and women, both skilled and unskilled. The jolas has a strong interest for the participants, but produces a spectacle of little aesthetic relevance from the observer's point of view. In the joko, alternatively, the interest of the player's defense of his interests is bolstered by the awareness of the spectator because of the uncertainty of the contest; therefore, it is common that the symbolic and fun faceoff is reinforced by bets and by a process of athletic identification with one of the contenders, which benefits the spectacle. The business of betting, admission, and publicity of the Basque pelota ball games demand the use of the joko, which is transparent from the spectator's point of view; the jolas does not have a place in this world of identities in conflict.

Reflecting on the evolution of the rules of the joko Basque pelota ball games requires one to consider closely the eventual spectator of the game: the process of generating identification with one of the contenders can be key. The majority of academics agree that ancient games of handball were the origin of Basque pelota ball, as well as the popular sport of tennis, among others. The ancient games are characterized by utilizing the rule of the *raya*, *chaza*, *chasse*, or *arraya*, to continue gaining a spatial advantage in preparation to winning one point or fifteen, and they survived, in their diverse local forms (*laxoa, guante, pasaka, boteluzea, errebote*), to the end of the nineteenth century. These ancestral games satisfied all the needs of the locals with respect to transparency of the rules, identification with one of the contenders, the desire to pay to watch the contest, and to bet. The population migrations of the industrial era changed the profile of the game's spectators, which meant that the transparent and clear rules which the locals were used to were confusing to new arrivals. The rules of play being too complex for the non-initiated kept a considerable group of the population from appreciating the spectacle and the business that could be generated. The struggle between the ancient longitudinal games, that is, with contestants facing each other, and the games of *blé* that featured players next to each other and throwing against a wall, was as brutal as the one that took place between the rural traditional cultures and the new industrial society.

Besides altering the position of the *raya* facing each other, the blé ball games saw additional changes to appeal to the spectator of the industrial era. The first characteristic was that the game utilized less field of play, which made the game's action concentrated in a smaller terrain to facilitate the spectacle and resolution of conflicting plays. The equipment of the game, tools, and ball, was also diversified to please the spectator. The incorporation of closed buildings with fields with left walls made the game even more transparent, since the bounce of the ball on the wall resent it toward the spectator bleachers, which strengthened the spectacle, encouraged higher entry fees, and spurred betting.

The Basque emigration at the start of the twentieth century expanded the taste for an appealing and transparent game that allowed for betting in Havana, Milan, or Miami, adapted to the needs of each location. Jai alai in the US, as well as in other locations outside of Basque Country, use the system of *quiniela* wagering, which further breaks the athletic duality of the traditional Basque joko, to incorporate a greater percentage of chance in the contest and less identification of bettor/spectator with the players.

The evolution of the joko ball games is a reflection of the evolution of the society in which they are played; after all, the games have always incorporated the characteristics of Basque community life.

—Joseba Etxebeste-Otegi, Physical and Sport Education, University of the Basque Country (EHU-UPV)

How did jai alai begin? Although the exact origins are obscure, jai alai, Basque for "happy festival," refers to the three-walled court of front, back, and left walls, and the sport of throwing and catching the rubber-core ball with the wicker cesta—a combination of speed and spectacular plays.

One origin story postulates that jai alai began in 1857 when Gantxiki Harotcha, a potato farmer in the French Basque town of St. Pée-sur-Nivelle, scooped potatoes from his field with a deep curved shovel and flung the shovelful into a harvest basket. He daydreamed, perhaps wondering how he could beat his neighbor on Sundays afternoons when everyone in the village came to see the men compete in games. His favorite handball game had changed. Now he wore on his right hand a heavy, rather pricey leather glove reinforced with iron. It required a lot of effort to strike and propel the ball to the front wall and off a sidewall. Could he hurl the ball faster and farther with a light basket made from woven strips of wicker?

He picked up the farm basket and cut and shaped it into a sort of basket glove with a strap to secure it to his hand. His was a practical solution to a tactical issue.

An alternative story explains that a thirteen-year-old Basque boy town from the town of St. Pée improvised his mother's flower basket. Was his name Gantxiki Harotcha, the same as the potato farmer, or Juanito Dithurbide, or a combination of the two names, Gantchiki Dithurbide? Did he sprain his hand, or was his hand fine but the leather glove too heavy, or was he unable to afford the glove? Most agree the boy dumped the flowers out of his mother's curved flower basket, tied the light basket to his hand with a string, ran to the neighborhood court to join his friends, and flung the ball. His father must have concluded that this innovation was amazing, because he set up shop to make this new throwing device. Or, some say the enterprising boy made his own baskets, sold them to his friends, and only later did the adults pick up on his invention.

Regardless of its nebulous beginning, the christened *chistera*, straighter and shorter than today's cesta, evolved into the distinctive symbol of the grace and power of jai alai. The ball flew from the refined cesta.

Jai alai was new, and future jai alai players honed their skills on handball courts scattered throughout the Basque Country. In the small town of Marquina in the mountainous Spanish Basque region, the town fathers invested their money where their passions were, Basque Ball. They commissioned Martin Usatorre to construct the Marquina Fronton, later known as the "University of Jai Alai," the breeding ground for talented players. As early as 1798 the original walled court may have accommodated an early form of handball similar to the French jeu de paume, face-to-face on opposing sides. But by the early 1800s the players had switched to different specialties of court handball. Now they faced the front wall and hit the hard rubber ball barehanded. In time the players adapted their equipment to throw and catch the ball far and strong. They switched to leather gloves reinforced with iron (*guante*), flat bats, and wooden paddles. They threw the ball out of the small basket chistera, and ultimately from the *gran chistera*, the cesta of jai alai fame. With each equipment innovation the Marquina Fronton responded with yet another adjustment to the configuration of the court playing area.

In 1928 Marquina enlarged the municipal fronton with a long range court and three walls specifically designed to play cesta punta, already marketed internationally as jai alai. Here the utilitarian yet landmark fronton set the stage for professional jai alai—with a brief hiatus. During the Spanish Civil War that lasted from 1936 until 1939, the troops of the faction loyal to the republic used the three-story fronton as a military garage. Troops of the opposing rebel faction bombed it. And Marquina rebuilt.

By the beginning of the twentieth century, jai alai as an organized sport traveled. "Wherever they (the Basques) went, they took their customs and traditions with them, as well as their religion and beloved pelota," says historian Carmelo Urza. This included Havana, Cuba; Buenos Aires, Argentina; Manila, Philippines; Tientsin, China; and Miami, Florida. Eventually, when sports organizers recognized the commercial potential of international jai alai, the owners of the frontons wanted and demanded the best, Basque professional jai alai players . . . as Basque and professional as José Goitia.

Born in 1947, Goitia grew up in Marquina (spelled Markina in his native Basque language), then a town of about three thousand residents in a valley in the foothills of the Pyrenees Mountains in northeastern Spain. Home was an old farmhouse adjacent to an idle stone mill on the banks of a stream in the center of town. Home is also the continuity of his family, his clan under the umbrella of the farmhouse where he was born, Abisu. Even if the physical homestead is gone, Goitia is a Basque who always belongs to his house, his *etxea*.

"I do not remember how old I was when I started to play jai alai, but I do know that cestas were among my first 'toys,'" says Goitia. "In one of the rooms in my house there was a big chest containing some old cestas that belonged to my uncles, who were professionals and stars of the sport. Two of my uncles were playing in Havana, Cuba, and another in Mexico City. There were also two small cestas that had belonged to my older cousin."

After school Goitia ran home and joined his friends to play jai alai at the outdoor court, a type of sandlot jai alai. Sometimes three or four of them rented an indoor amateur court at the Marquina Fronton for an hour. "It did not take much for my friends and me to start playing games. Even a shoe box, pressed and held on one end, used to be a good substitute for a cesta," says Goitia.

Often he detoured and played a quick game of handball against a stone wall on a dirt playing area. He pretended he played with his cesta strapped to his wrist, whipped the ball against the uneven wall, and in one continuous sweep returned it on the bounce. Good practice for a future jai alai player, a pelotari.

Before Goitia was sixteen years old he left home to play professional jai alai in Zaragoza, Spain. At home decent paying jobs were scarce and options few, while jai alai provided an upward career path. Two years later in 1966 when he was eighteen years old he signed a contract to play in Dania, Florida, where the salary was lucrative and the playing season long, between nine and ten months each year. "Here was the beginning of what I had dreamed since I was a kid," says Goitia.

Figure 2.3. "I was fourteen years old playing amateur *partido* during ceremonies at Marquina Fronton to honor Erdoza Menor, one of the greatest players of all time." Jai alai player José Goitia, Marquina, Spain, 1962. Courtesy of José Goitia.

This is the distinctly Basque jai alai of José Goitia's world. At first, some Basque sports fans voiced their opinion that the players of this new version of handball did not play fair. Why did the players catch and hold the ball in the curve of the basket and throw at will? Let them use their bare hand, the natural way. In 1909 in San Sebastián, Spain, the audience walked out in the middle of the jai alai game. Yet jai alai was fast and thrilling and suave. With standardized playing rules in place the Basques adopted jai alai as their own creation.

This is the jai alai, part aerobatic dance and part superb athleticism, that the Basques modernized and exported. Worldwide it became the most widely known version of Basque Ball outside of the Basque region. Fans and promoters touted jai alai as "the fastest game in the world."

THE "FASTEST GAME IN THE WORLD"

3

On Friday evening, August 3, 1979, at Newport Jai Alai in Newport, Rhode Island, jai alai player José Ramón Areitio broke the world record for the fastest ball thrown in a sport.

From the street, passersby on Admiral Kalbfus Road observed a three-story windowless building painted with the words "Hi-Li" across the gray concrete walls. In 1976, Boston contractor Arthur Silvester Sr. introduced jai alai to the New England summer resort. For Silvester, who also owned Palm Beach Jai Alai, professional jai alai was increasingly big business in the American sports market. Here was an opportunity to gain a foothold in the metro Northeast and provide work for his players during the Florida off-season. For Rhode Island state legislators, jai alai attracted tourists and provided an opportunity to reap tax revenue from the specially enacted legalized gambling law for jai alai.

On this night a sellout crowd of three thousand fans placed their bets for their favorite player to win, place, or show, and took their seats to watch athletes hurl the game ball at speeds that could potentially injure or even kill. In the early days of Miami Jai Alai in the 1930s, before the advent of protective helmets, a player known as Ramos died when his backcourt doubles partner returned the ball as it rebounded off the rear wall. The ball struck frontcourter Ramos in the back of the head, and he died a couple of days later. The fans did not hope for a disaster, but the perilous ball certainly added excitement.

How fast did the jai alai ball travel? Was jai alai really the "fastest game in the world"? At the time, the fastest tennis serve was about 153 mph at impact off the racket, and the best baseball players pitched a fastball at 100 mph.

"Faster than lightning," the promoters proclaimed at the jai alai games in 1938 at the Hippodrome in New York City. Preposterous. Yet everyone who sat in the stands at a jai alai game and followed the ball in play agreed: the ball exploded with speed when the best players threw it from the curved cesta with the full force of their body. Some said as fast as 140–150 mph, others in the range of 180 mph.

The management at Newport Jai Alai proposed a contest between two of their players to clock the speed of the ball. To be sure, this was a public relations event aimed to create interest. Yet the point was if they validated the speed of the ball and the player beat the world record, then jai alai proved itself.

Between the fifth and sixth games of regular play, José Ramón Areitio and his teammate Tomas Ovarvide walked onto the court followed by Portsmouth, Rhode Island, Deputy Police Chief Madison Bailey carrying a police radar gun. While Areitio and Ovarvide alternated competition throws to the front granite wall, Bailey stood to the side and held the radar gun in line with the traveling ball. On Areitio's final attempt, Bailey shouted, 188 mph, a record! The crowd cheered and then rushed from their seats to the cashiers to wager a last minute bet on the upcoming game. "How to Break World Record," reported the *Newport Daily News*'s Rick McGowan. The Guinness Book of World Records officially entered the Newport claim: the fastest-moving ball sport was jai alai.

The controversy began. What did the Guinness book editors use as their comparative standard? Throughout the history of jai alai was 188 mph the fastest-traveling ball? For no one electronically measured the speed of the ball thrown by star players during high levels of play. And allowing for technological inaccuracy, how verifiable was the speed measured by the radar gun used in 1979? Today, the accuracy of radar guns has improved.

Veteran jai alai players, the Basque stalwarts, considered the Newport event a cheap publicity stunt, offensive to the Basque tradition of the art of jai alai. Yet "this is indisputable, the pelota (ball) moved very fast. It's too bad we didn't have an accurate means of measuring the speed of the pelota during an actual game. That's when breathtaking speeds were attained. In the heat of action, when some of the really hard throwers got the adrenaline pumping, the ball looked like a blur," says Bob Heussler, former public relations manager at Milford Jai Alai in Connecticut.

In the history of jai alai, it was this solid rubber ball, a product of the Mesoamerican ancient ball game, that changed the way the Basques played their traditional group of handball sports, Basque pelota. The "fastest game in the world" began with the amazing bouncing rubber ball.

In his sixteenth-century chronicle *De orbe novo* (On the New World), Peter Martyr d'Anghiera, an Italian-born Spanish historian, told the story of how the indigenous peoples of the tropical Americas made rubber game balls from "the juice of the vine that clambers over the trees, as hop vines clamber among the hedges." Because the Mesoamericans figured out a way to extract a natural polymer called *hule*, or rubber, from a native rubber plant, they could make an elastic ball alive with motion.

Martyr scrutinized the letters and documents of the early Spanish conquistadors who trekked through the lowlands and highlands of pre-Hispanic Mesoamerica, present-day Mexico and Central America, to convert and colonize. He interviewed returning adventurers. He told the story of Christopher Columbus landing on the shores of the Caribbean islands and the march across Mexico by Hernán Cortés. He described teams of Aztec ballplayers in Tenochtitlán, Mexico, on opposing sides of a specially designed court playing a competitive sport with a bouncing rubber ball. "The natives are most skillful players at this exercise, catching the ball on their shoulders, elbows, heads, rarely their hands, and sometimes their hips, if their opponents throw when their backs are turned."

PELOTA MIXTECA IN OAXACA, MEXICO: AN ARCHAEOLOGIST'S PERSPECTIVE

In 2008, I was sitting in the Zócalo, Oaxaca's principal plaza and meeting space, discussing research projects for dissertation research with archaeologist friends. When I mentioned my interest in ball courts, one of them leaned over and said,

"You know they still play the ball game today?" I was instantly intrigued—what an amazing opportunity to bridge the archaeological record with the ethnographic present! I knew that if I was going to do research on the pre-Hispanic ball game in Oaxaca, I had to investigate the *pelota Mixteca*, or Mixtec rubber ball, as it is known. Given the political and religious importance we often ascribe to the pre-Hispanic game, I especially wanted to know what significance the modern game had for the people who played and watched it.

The first exhibition match I ever attended was a *torneo* or tournament held in honor of the patron saint of San Antonio Arrazola, a small town located on the southwestern side of Oaxaca. Watching my first pelota Mixteca match as an outside observer was at times a bewildering experience, as the field was fairly crowded and activity was constant. The tournament was played round-robin style, with several teams of five—*las quintas*—waiting to rotate in to play their set. The *saquero* initiates the match by bouncing the rubber ball against the *botadora*, an inclined playing stone, then striking it with a heavy leather glove. The ball is then bounced back and forth across the playing field. Players waiting their turn often stood on the sidelines or walked along the playing field, yelling encouragement or disparaging comments at rivals and friends alike. There were also referees or *chaceros*, one for each set of quintas playing. Disagreements over rules and game points broke out here and there, resolved by animated shouting and hand gestures. Audience members also frequently got involved, trading insults with players and commenting frequently on game play. Shots of mezcal, the local liquor made from the *maguey* plant (a type of agave), were shared among players and spectators. It was a festive, celebratory atmosphere not unlike an American-style tailgate party at a football stadium.

While pelota Mixteca may not have the same overtly religious symbolism and rituals that it had in the pre-Hispanic past, as a game it still has significant cultural and social meaning for players. Communities that still play invite teams from other towns to come compete for cash prizes and local prestige. To accept an invitation is an honor, and to not show up affects your *calidad moral*, or your reputation. Playing is about giving and receiving, hosts and guests inviting each other in a cyclical exchange of *diversión* (fun), gambling, friendly competition, and showmanship. One player summed it up best by describing the game thus—*Pelota Mixteca es como la guelaguetza, si me das, te doy* ("*Pelota Mixteca* is like *guelaguetza* [a tradition of reciprocity and obligation], if you give to me, I give to you."). While disagreements do occur, rivalries are sustained, and fights break out—competition can be cutthroat, after all—above all pelota Mixteca links communities together in complicated and dynamic ways.

In many ways the game represents the survival and persistence of pre-Hispanic practices in the face of persecution and oppression. Despite attempts to repress native ball games by the Spanish, Oaxaqueños maintained their traditions, adopting and adapting the game to create a modern twist on a cherished sport.

—Marijke Maurine Stoll, Archaeologist

The Spanish, accustomed to dull game balls made of wood, leather, or cloth, were astonished. Was the bouncing ball possessed by evil spirits, the work of the devil? "I do not understand how these heavy balls are so elastic that when they touch the ground, even though lightly thrown, they spring

Figure 3.1. Decorated leather gloves, often studded with nails, used to catch and throw the ball in pelota Mixteca, an ancient handball game. Oaxaca, Mexico, 2014. Courtesy of Marijke Maurine Stoll.

into the air with the most incredible leaps," said one Spanish explorer.

What seemed extraordinary to the Spanish was ordinary to the indigenous people of the New World. The Mesoamericans lived in the midst of that natural resource. In Mexico, *Castilla elastica*, one of two thousand rubber plant species that produce latex containing rubber particles, grows abundantly in the tropical lowlands of Chiapas, Yucatan, Tabasco, and Veracruz. By 1600 BC, Mesoamericans were processing the natural rubber substance, 3,500 years before Charles Goodyear developed vulcanized rubber, a chemical process to convert rubber into a durable, viable commercial material.

Mesoamericans used rubber to attach stone implements to wooden tool handles, to make drumstick tips, and to form shields as protection from an enemy warrior's arrows. They smeared it on ear and lip wounds and concocted medicinal applications for sore throats and stomach problems. They molded small rubber gods called *ulteteo*. Predominantly, though, they produced solid and compact rubber balls: small irregular-shaped balls for religious offerings and heavy regular-shaped ones with a bounce for game balls.

The people of the ancient civilizations of the Olmec, Maya, and Aztec were particularly masters at making hard, bouncing rubber balls, the fundamental element of their ritual and political ball game. How did they harvest latex, the raw liquid rubber, to make their rubber balls?

The early Maya ball makers of Chiapas, Mexico, worked in the lowlands jungle where the rubber trees, some eighty feet tall, grew wild. Generally, when the latex flowed at its peak from around March to June, the men cut a vertical channel in the bark of the tree. Along the vertical channel they scored diagonal channels, the white latex dripped, and the containers filled. For two to five hours, the men collected the latex and strained it to remove insects.

Then they mixed. They ingeniously created a formula of two different ingredients: the latex combined with the juice crushed from a local species of the morning glory vine (*Ipomoea alba*). By itself natural latex was a sticky liquid that dried into an unworkable brittle solid. The juices added plasticity and elasticity. After about ten minutes of stirring, the latex mixture coagulated into a solid mass of rubber. The men had several minutes before it hardened to shape the rubber into the desired form and size, depending on the region and the type of game. Now they had a compact, bouncy rubber ball fundamental to the Mesoamerican ball game and Basque Ball.

In another place, Miami, Florida, at another time, the twenty-first century, in a small windowless room on the second floor of Miami Jai Alai, now part of a casino, Miguel Altuna from Basque Spain and Clemente Garcia from Mexico

Figure 3.2. The four stages of making the jai alai ball.

sat side by side before a wooden table producing game balls for jai alai. Each worked on his individually constructed ball with hand tools: a heavy-duty stapler, yarn, leather-point needle and ball of nylon thread, knife, and ball press. The goatskin was from England; the Virgin de Para rubber from Brazil.

Around and around Altuna and Garcia rolled narrow strips of rubber produced from liquid rubber poured over a flat surface and dried into thin sheets. Each had the "touch" and knew instinctively the point when he held in his hand a core of the desired size and weight. And then he weighed it on the scale and smiled as if he had won a contest with himself for accuracy. He smoothed out air pockets with his fingers before covering the dense core with yarn and applying the first layer of damp goatskin. When it was dry, he sewed the second layer of goatskin over the ball and flattened the seams together in the press to give the ball an even bounce and clean sound.

Figure 3.3. Clemente Garcia and Miguel Altuna, ballmakers at Miami Jai Alai, 2013.

The average jai alai ball weighs approximately 4.4 ounces and is 2.5 inches in diameter. The players refer to a new ball as "cold" and "dead." For when the rubber is cool, the bounce is softer and the play slower than with a used ball. But during a game when the ball repeatedly bounces off the floor or strikes the wall, the long molecular strands of the rubber become compressed. As the ball comes off the wall, the molecules spring back into shape like a rubber band. Some of the energy is absorbed into the ball as heat. The harder the player throws the ball from his cesta, the more the strands are compressed when the ball hits the hard surface. Now the ball is "hot" and "tight," the bounce high.

The best jai alai players know a new or used ball affects the way they play the game. The server selects a ball and shows it to his opponent. "Look to the ball and say, I know what kind of player he is. Does he select a new coated ball

Figure 3.4. Francisco Churruca at a charity game in 1957 at La Habana Fronton, "playing with those considered to be the best players of the time: Orbea, Salsamendi III, and Guarita." Jai alai player Francisco Churruca, Havana, Cuba. Courtesy of Francisco Churruca.

because he prefers soft shots with a low, dying bounce? Comes my turn to serve, I choose a ball depending on my opponent's weakness or skill," says one of the great professional players, Francisco Maria Churruca Iriondo Azpiazu Alcorta—or simply "Churruca."

The goatskin covering rips, though, from the high-impact play during a performance. "Sometimes I broke about four or five a day," says Churruca. At the time, every fronton set aside a repair shop where the repairman (*pelotero*) was on call during the games to stitch a new goat skin covering. "Now the re-stitched ball is like a new ball, soft bounce. Change in play," says Churruca.

For two or three seasons, the re-covered jai alai ball

remains in play until the ball is simply too worn to meet quality standards. Quality counts. In 1974, a thief reportedly stole 467 jai alai balls valued at over eighteen thousand dollars from the Miami Jai Alai fronton. It was said that the owners of Miami Jai Alai requested the Federal Bureau of Investigation's assistance, although ultimately the owners paid a ransom to recover the game balls. "The importance of the theft lay in the impossibility in the short term of finding replacement balls of similar quality," says author José Perallón. Unlike the process for making manufactured, uniform baseballs, there was no machine to mass produce the custom-made jai alai game balls.

Bounce high, bounce low, travel fast or slow, the right game ball thrown from the right cesta by a talented player is exciting. Jai alai is not a contact sport—no tackles on the football field or brawls on the ice hockey rink. The violence is in the hard rubber ball gathered and thrown from the long curved wicker cesta designed to increase the speed and power of the ball.

●

"A good player worries for his cesta. I took care of my cesta like it was food for me. Each day I measured it because it was made from chestnut wood and could be affected by the weather. Too dry and it might become brittle. Too damp, the wood swells and the cesta gets longer. I wanted it to be the same length and width every day I played, so sometimes I added a wicker piece. I got used to my make of cesta; it suited me. When I threw the ball from my cesta, I knew how the ball would fly out, not too fast, not too slow," says Churruca.

"If players could change cestas in a match, they would pick a damp one for catching, because the damp reeds are more pliable, and they would use a dry one for throwing because it has less friction," said amateur player Katherine Hines Herrington. During the 1960s and '70s, Herrington managed public relations for Dania Jai Alai in Dania, Florida. But after work was different. On an amateur court, mostly among men, she learned to play jai alai. She knew about cestas.

"Buying a cesta is like buying your wife gold jewelry . . . valuable, expensive and personal," says Churruca. The frontcourt player wants a light, relatively small cesta, easy to handle as he moves quickly to reach and return the ball as it rebounds off the front granite wall. The backcourt player needs a big and strong cesta with a deep pocket to hurl the ball back to the front wall. A cesta weighs between fifteen and twenty ounces. It wears out, sometimes as often as fifteen times a year, and then the player pays at least three hundred dollars for a replacement.

Making a cesta is an art. At Miami Jai Alai, Carlos Campos creates custom-made cestas according to the Basque tradition. He steam-bends the chestnut frame and ribs planed to $1/16$th inch thick and 1 inch wide. Cut the trees at full moon, the Basque old-timers claim, and then the chestnut wood grown in tree groves in Spain bends into form without breaking. Over the chestnut skeleton, Campos weaves thin reeds from the Pyrenees Mountains, patiently shaping and smoothing every interwoven reed with a piece of glass. When Campos is finished, he sews a leather glove to the outside of the cesta. He has worked with pride for over fifty years.

Modern cesta, which originated in 1857 as the small basket scoop chistera in the Basque Country, took on a life of its own in Buenos Aires, Argentina. In 1886, Melchor Guruceaga traveled from his native Basque Country to compete in the game of chistera, similar to but not as fast and challenging as jai alai. The players threw and caught the ball with a light basket made of strips of chestnut wood, too short and shallow to match the speed and power of the future cesta.

It was in Argentina that the left-handed Basque player Chiquito de Eibar (Indalecio Sarasqueta) captured the attention of the South Americans by defeating one of their own, Paysandú (Pedro Zabaleta) from Uruguay. Sometimes Chiquito played the sport with his bare hand, other times with glove or chistera, but always Chiquito hit the ball against the wall in a fast and furious game. The Argentine people applauded and asked for more. The Argentinians loved their sports and wagering, and here were the Basques, tough and highly competitive athletes who brought their varieties of Basque Ball with them when they immigrated to Argentina.

When Melchor Guruceaga stepped off the ship onto the dock, he stepped into a world of compatriots, part of the large-scale immigration from the Basque region to Argentina. The exodus began in 1492 when twenty-three Basques sailed with Christopher Columbus across the Atlantic Ocean from Spain to the New World. The Spanish came, conquered, and colonized, and the trade network initiated by Basque shipbuilders, financiers, and merchants spread the word about Argentina. In 1580, Basque native Juan de Garay founded Buenos Aires.

First came the people from towns and cities; later, there was emigration from the Basque countryside. Once Argentina declared its independence from Spain in 1816, it actively welcomed and recruited immigrants, particularly the Basques with their strong work ethic, to populate and energize their new country. In the Basque Country, Argentine agents would even present their sales pitch to people as they were leaving Catholic Mass on Sundays. "Migration became a business, with the specialists providing loans, dealing with legal paperwork, and providing transportation to ports, inns, and places to eat and stay while waiting for ships and transatlantic voyages," says historian Gloria Totoricagüena.

Between 1857 and 1940, more than two million Spanish people—according to estimates—immigrated to Argentina, mostly from Galicia and the Basque Country. The Basques immigrated to escape the political domination of Spain after the two Carlist Civil Wars, 1833–1839 and 1872–1876, and the assault on Basque culture from General Francisco Franco, who came into power in 1939 at the end of the Spanish Civil War (1936–1939). They immigrated to start businesses, run banks, enter politics, purchase land, graze sheep, and raise cattle. And to revolutionize the sport of jai alai in a place distant from the Basque Country.

Melchor Guruceaga was not the Chiquito de Eibar of Argentina fame, but Guruceaga played with competence and "an electric spark." Most important, he was smart and innovative, attributes that made a difference when in 1887 he fractured his wrist and did not regain his normal strength to throw the ball hard from the short chistera. He needed to get back to work. How could he propel the ball with less wrist motion? What would give him an advantage over the other players? How could he play a powerful backhand?

Guruceaga shepherded the cesta into its next phase of evolution—the long, narrow, curved, and deep-channeled cesta that is distinctive to jai alai. Guruceaga gathered the ball in the hollowed-out area of his innovation and swung his backhand. The ball then spun with a curve of more than five feet. He scooped up the ball, allowed it to roll to one end of the basket, and then hurled it off the tip with greater force than with the glove or chistera. He was ready to take his invention public.

Guruceaga was a short man, the cesta was long, and the fans laughed. But when he launched the ball from the new cesta, the ball flew "like a bullet from a rifle," says author José Perallón. Guruceaga's converts dubbed the innovative cesta "The Mauser," after the German repeating rifle designed to hit its target at high velocity.

Jai alai seemed destined to thrive in its host country of Argentina. "But its reign of acute popularity was lamentably short in Buenos Aires," wrote British traveler William Henry Koebel in 1907. A group of Spanish players "entered into the spirit of Argentine wagering, and the bets which they made with their hosts upon the results of the game were weighty." Koebel was not above gossip and rumored that the players fleeced the locals, who sent them packing back to Spain. Yet once Argentine entrepreneurs recognized the potential profit of professional jai alai and operated commercial frontons in the cities, jai alai was there to stay awhile. But Koebel was correct about its vulnerability. Jai alai spawned a rival court game with an Argentine twist, *pelota a paleta* (paddleball), now called *paleta Argentina*.

The story of paleta in Argentina is the story of Gabriel Martirén, who in 1905 was a French Basque dairy farmer from Burzaco, twenty miles from Buenos Aires. He wanted to relax with his employees by playing jai alai. Missing was the cesta, an expensive piece of equipment. He would have to locate a cesta maker who imported the raw materials or order a cesta from Spain. So he improvised, working with what he had on hand, the shoulder blade left over from butchering one of his cows.

Martirén practiced hitting the ball with the "shovel blade." He then asked a local carpenter to construct a similar paddle from wood. Probably at first he and his friends played with a stripped tennis ball, later replaced with the proper goatskin ball. During an early game of paleta played on the short handball court at the village Gaucha Republic hotel, one journalist wrote that "betting was strong." Martirén's legacy is carved on his tombstone, where he is remembered as the inventor of paleta.

Both jai alai and paleta are fast and exciting sports since the players strike the ball against the wall with the specialized cesta or paddle. In both the games, the players run up and down a defined walled court, although the paleta court is shorter than the jai alai court. The difference is that the rural Argentine people worked with simplified equipment of paleta for their impromptu games. At one point, due to a rubber shortage during World War II, farmers and herders even played with a cloth ball, reverting to the dull game ball in its original ancient form.

Ultimately, rural and urban Argentinians identified with paleta as an Argentine sport, albeit created by a Basque immigrant. Paleta became hugely popular throughout Argentina until today, when the pride of Argentina rides on the international sport of soccer.

Still, the impressive game of jai alai left its imprint on Argentina, while also traveling back to its home in the Basque Country . . . and further.

4

JAI ALAI IN CUBA

"What the theater is to New York jai alai is to Havana. Everyone goes to the game and bets on the players. There are theaters—several of them—and usually during the greater part of the winter there is some kind of attraction at each, but these attractions pale into nothingness before the greater one of jai alai," said journalist Dorothy Stanhope in 1904. Cuba's fascination with jai alai began with the Spanish colonization of Cuba. Since Cuba was part of New Spain, the presence of the Spanish influenced how the Cubans spoke, ate, worshipped, learned, worked, and played.

"The most beautiful land that human eyes have ever seen," said Christopher Columbus, guiding the *Santa Maria* along the northeast coastline of tropical Cuba, in and out of river channels on his first exploratory voyage to the New World in 1492. He set foot on land at the present site of Baracoa, stuck the flag of Spain in the sand, and claimed the island for his angel investor, Queen Isabella of Spain. In 1511 Diego Velázquez de Cuéllar and a group of colonists established the first Spanish settlement at Baracoa. Three years later the Spanish founded Havana—"San Cristóbal de La Habana."

From 1519 until 1898 the *penisulares*, resident colonists born in Spain, and the *criollos*, those who were Cuban-born of Spanish ancestry, told the story of Cuba. They governed, taxed, soldiered, and mastered large sugar and coffee plantations. They drank Catalonia wine, ate pork from imported swine, bathed in the sea salt baths of Baños de Mar, and built their homes around enclosed courtyards. They shot pool in smoky billiard rooms, won or lost at cards, urged on their favorite birds at cockfights, and applauded the kill of the bull by Spanish matadors at the Plaza de Toros.

The ways of sport in Cuba reflected the ways of the motherland of Spain. As customs changed, the distinguishing features of sports changed. By the eighteenth century, the favorite sport of Spain was a spectator sport, bullfighting, with plenty of betting.

Gambling was a tradition in Cuba. Cubans bet on cockfights, bullfights, billiards, dice-throwing, the lottery, and ball games. They wagered for fun, for the challenge, and for money. Gambling ameliorated a poverty-drab or leisure-boring life.

In 1771, alarmed by the poverty and corruption in Cuba, King Carlos II attempted to make gambling illegal in all the Spanish colonies (but not in Spain). "There is not a city, town or district in the island of Cuba where this devouring cancer is absent," said statesman José Antonio Saco in *La vagancia en Cuba* (Vagrancy in Cuba). Poor roads, poor homes, poor schools, vagrancy, destitute children—gambling was the source of the country's ills. Close the gambling houses, ban the betting games, control the social clubs and the daily lotteries, Saco proposed. Instead, visit a museum or walk for recreation. The wealthy, the military, investors, owners, government officials, and the ordinary citizen said, "No." Gambling did not go away. In 1859 Boston traveler Richard Henry Dana visited Cuba and observed, "Havana is flooded with lottery-ticket vendors. They infest every eating-house and public way, and vex you at dinner, in your walks and rides."

Jai alai traveled to Cuba with the Basques, who transported their beloved Basque Ball with its subculture of betting. Against the churchyard wall of Spanish Roman Catholic missions, Dominican and Franciscan priests played Basque handball, the predecessor of jai alai, for a simple wager of a bottle of wine or rum. Against the uneven public-building walls in the streets of Havana, Basque seaman on shore leave threw the ball, pitting their best players against each other, hoping to win a few extra coins. On the plaza in residential neighborhoods, Basque immigrants built playing courts with a front and left-handed wall, attracting the locals who joined the betting.

On December 12, 1790, the influential Havana newspaper, *Papel Periodico de La Habana*, publicly announced a professional Basque handball match on an official playing court. The advertisement ran like this: "Today! In the 'Real Factoria de Pelota!' You will see nine accomplished Basque players compete in a great game of ball!" The reporter warned his readers: the players are competitive, the game is thrilling, the betting intense . . . in the height of passion, do not get carried away with your emotions and create a public disorder. No throwing hats, walking sticks, or coins on the court. No fighting with the judges, your neighbor, or bookmaker. But the audience ignored the advice.

Interest in the sport grew. On October 23, 1881, in the Vedado neighborhood of Havana, players from Havana and

Bolondrón in the Matanzas province competed in a match of rivals presided over by Ramón Blanco, Spanish captain general of Cuba. The game began as *pelota a mano*, played with the bare hand; it ended as chistera, played with an early version of the wicker basket to throw and catch the ball. Play was fast, and the hard rubber ball rocketed off the wall with a resounding crack. The men stood up from their seats, shouted, shook their fists, and threw gold pieces at the player who scored the winning point. The women sat in the back in the ladies' section, eating ice cream and drinking wine, listening to music played by the popular Chapelgorri band, and admiring the handsome athletes leap and twist.

As the game of Basque handball evolved into the wild sporting spectacle of cesta punta enhanced with the innovative long and curved cesta, enterprisers who promoted the sport in Cuba recognized the global value of a marketable brand name. No doubt motivated by the thought of an international string of jai alai organizations, the Cuban promoters, so it is said, adopted the name of jai alai, "happy festival" in Basque, evoking the image of a celebrated sport performed on festival days in the exotic European land.

Basque Ball—hand, glove, paddle, or basket—was there to stay in Cuba, with or without Spain. In 1868 Spain's ever-faithful colony, *Cuba la sempre fiel*, rebelled against the established Old World order. A month after the Revolutionists in Spain forced Queen Isabella II to abdicate her crown, Cuba responded with its own homegrown independence movement. Thus began the onset of thirty years of Cuba's exhaustive and debilitating on-and-off armed struggle for independence. Despite their persistence, the Cubans were unable to expel Spain from Cuba until the United States intervened during the Spanish-American War in 1898.

On February 15, 1898, the USS *Maine*, the United States Navy battleship stationed in Cuba to support the Cuban revolt against the Spaniards and protect American business interests, blew up in Havana Harbor, killing 260 crew members. The United States blamed Spain, and two months later President William McKinley declared war.

The Spanish-American War, fought in the Spanish territories of Cuba, Puerto Rico, Guam, and the Philippines, was a relatively short war, beginning on April 25, 1898, and ending on December 10, 1898, with the signing of the Treaty of Paris. It was in Cuba that the United States forces, including Teddy Roosevelt's volunteer Rough Riders and the African American Buffalo Soldiers, defeated the Spanish at the decisive battle of San Juan and Kettle Hill.

"For six days the army was encamped on either side of the trail (from Siboney to Santiago) for three miles back from the outposts. The regimental camps touched each other, and all day long the pack-trains carrying the day's rations passed up and down between them. The trail was a sunken wagon road . . . the banks of the trail were three or four feet high, and when it rained it was converted into a huge gutter, with sides of mud, and with a liquid mud a foot deep between them," reported American war correspondent Richard Harding Davis.

On June 30, 1898, about fifteen thousand troops broke camp and moved forward. Infantry, cavalry, artillery soldiers, Cuban generals, US officers, reporters, and photographers stumbled and slipped toward the hills of San Juan (San Juan Heights). "It was as though fifteen regiments were encamped along the sidewalks of Fifth Avenue and were all ordered at the same moment to move into it and march downtown," said Davis.

The Spanish brought more than the game of jai alai to Cuba. The American advance "was met with a murderous hail from Mauser rifles, which temporarily stayed the forward movement." This was the rapid-firing Mauser that jai alai fans appropriated as a nickname to describe the revolutionary cesta created by Guruceaga, the Mauser basket cesta, as feared on the court as the rifle was on the battlefield.

The Mauser earned a deadly reputation among the American soldiers in the San Juan trenches. The Spanish fired five rapid smokeless rounds of ammunition from the Mauser rifle, while the American militia armed with Springfield rifles fired single shots, emitting clouds of black powder, a sure betrayal of their location on the battlefield. Still, the American troops charged. "The men held their guns pressed across their chests and stepped heavily as they climbed," said Davis. On July 1, 1898, the United States defeated the Spanish at San Juan Hill and Kettle Hill. "It Required True Courage," said the *New York Times*. The end of the Spanish-American War was imminent.

At noon on January 1, 1899, on the rock promontory of Morro Castle guarding the entrance to Havana Bay, soldiers lowered the Spanish flag and raised the United States flag. The official understanding was that Cuba had achieved its independence from Spain. But in reality the United States under the Platt Amendment installed a provisional military government for "the maintenance of a government adequate for the protection of life, property and individual liberty," with the promise of eventual withdrawal of the United States from Cuba "to leave the government and control of the island to its people."

After decades of fighting Spain, Cuba was devastated. Food and clothing were scarce, schools dysfunctional, the land ravaged, property owners in debt, commerce disrupted, and the political system unstable. It was America's responsibility to prepare the Cuban people "politically, mentally, and morally" for self-governing, said General Leonard Wood, the military governor of Cuba. "If we fail the nations of the world will hold Americans responsible." In the Governor's Palace in Havana General Wood sat at his desk on the requisitioned chair of the Spanish General "Weyler, The Damned," and administered. "The military government penetrated every area of Cuban social life." says historian Louis Pérez Jr. Even jai alai.

General Wood, one of the Rough Riders, was tall and broad-shouldered with a barrel chest, muscled arms, and thick hands. "He can walk like a bull moose; jump with the quickness of a cat; box, wrestle and fence like a professional," said journalist James Creelman. Creelman might have added that Wood was a natural for jai alai, moving fast around the court with muscular flexibility and throwing a well-placed ball with quick eye.

Jai alai entertained the American forces, but Wood was not satisfied to sit on the sidelines and watch. He learned to play the game. Jai alai became his activity of choice for after-hours relaxation. At the fronton he practiced with other amateurs or even a professional player or two who appreciated Wood's enthusiasm. So it happened that Wood, the jai alai fan, used his political authority to pave the way for a state-of-the-art commercial arena, the Jai Alai Fronton, in Havana.

"Consider, gentlemen, Jai Alai Fronton in Havana, the mecca of jai alai in North America," said Spanish businessman Tomás Mazzantini y Equía as he stood before the Havana Municipal Council in 1898. While the Spanish authorities took their time leaving Cuba, Mazzantini spent months in Cuba with his brother Luis, a famous Spanish matador who traveled the bullfighting circuit. Mazzantini had a vision, and it included jai alai and making money. In April 1898, Mazzantini applied for permission from the city to lease a large piece of land between Concordia, Lucena, Virtudes, and Marqués Streets to build a professional jai alai fronton.

Mazzantini proposed a sweet deal. He suggested he pay rent to the city and construct at his own expense an architect-designed sports arena. In ten years, he would give the land with the building back to the city. He added that tourists and fans would spend money in the city and locals would have job opportunities. Of course, the city had to supply extra police to keep order when the fans got out of control, but the exciting sport of jai alai would lift the worn-out Cubans' spirits.

The Municipal Authority concurred, granting permission to construct the jai alai fronton on city property with drinking and gambling privileges. Yet it was not ratified by the time of the American occupation. There were delays, mainly bureaucratic, some political, a few moral. The US military occupation muddied the legal waters with the "no new franchises or concessions" clause of the Foraker Act. They rejected the application. And so Wood, an American from New Hampshire, stepped in for the foreign sport of jai alai and appealed to the powers in Washington. Eventually, Washington granted a ten-year concession for the operation of the Jai Alai Fronton and authorized the games to begin. But the games had already begun. Several months before final approval from Washington, the contractors completed construction, Havana authorities officially consented, and

Figure 4.1. "Habana Jai Alai," Havana Fronton, Havana, Cuba, 1920s. Historic Postcard.

"the Basque game of jai alai, with license for betting" was in business.

Jai alai was in the news in Havana. Star pelotaris arrived by ship from Spain and South America to fill the game rosters for afternoon and evening matches. On a monthlong grand tour of Cuba in March 1902, First Daughter Alice Longworth Roosevelt and her chaperone "shopped, ate spicy Cuban food, and followed jai alai games closely," says historian Stacy Cordery.

Cubans, tourists, foreign businessmen, and American soldiers packed the Jai Alai Fronton to its capacity of several thousand, and they bet. Admission prices generally ranged from one dollar to five, from standing room to low-tier seats to second-tier family box seats reserved for fashionable and important people. In one of the box seats, General Wood entertained his guests. In the open space between the court and the seating area, bookmakers in white coats and red berets shouted the odds and accepted wagers of no less than four dollars. The Jai Alai Company collected ten percent of the winnings with profits estimated at fifteen thousand to twenty thousand dollars a month. "There was plenty of money afloat," said American journalist Henry Harrison Lewis. "[In a] game lasting not more than eight minutes . . . as high as twenty thousand dollars changed hands."

Jai alai was also in the news in Washington, DC. "Rathbone Charges Heard: Allegations against Gen. Wood Presented to the Senate Committee on Military Affairs," reported the *New York Times* on November 21, 1903. General Wood was in Washington, because United States military government had concluded its occupation of Cuba on May 20, 1902, and had transferred the Republic of Cuba to its people. Wood spent his time in Washington writing his Cuban report, meeting with his friend President Theodore Roosevelt, and preparing to leave for the Philippines where he was appointed governor general—if confirmed by the US Department of War and Congress. The business of Washington politics—enemies and power and money—potentially stood in his way.

The controversy began while General Wood was military governor and Major Estes Rathbone was director of the Cuban post office system. Allegedly, almost four hundred thousand dollars of surcharged stamps, due to be put out of circulation and burned, were preserved and sold. The Cuban Supreme Court confined Rathbone and Charles Neely, head of the Postal Finance Department, for embezzlement and refused them bail. Rathbone and Neely sat in prison until the court held a retrial and granted amnesty. Wood as military governor was embarrassed. Rathbone as prisoner was furious.

He blamed Wood for exceeding his authority by allowing the Cuban courts to retain jurisdiction and accused Wood of influencing the court. "There is no foundation for the charges," said United States Secretary of War Elihu Root.

Controversy between the two men continued in Washington, DC. When President Roosevelt promoted Wood to brigadier general and assigned him to lead the Philippines, Rathbone formally filed charges to the Senate Committee on Military Affairs to block the nomination. Among the specific allegations, Rathbone targeted jai alai.

This time jai alai was featured in Washington in the form of tabloid-style headlines. "New Scandal to Appear in the Wood Inquiry . . . 'Joker' Aided Concessions." The "joker" referred to Wood, the "fanatical jai alai devotee." The scandal was based on the official authorization Wood enacted for a ten-year concession to the Havana Jai Alai Fronton, "an immoral gambling concern." And the fact that Wood accepted a duty-free personal gift of a silver service from a delegation of Havana merchants associated with the jai alai fronton.

On March 17, 1904, General Wood took his cause live to the Senate to demonstrate the game. On the Senate floor during a closed-door executive session, the Senators wildly swung cestas to get the hang of throwing and catching with a curved basket strapped to the hand. "The spectacle of Senators clasping the basket racquets to their hands and gesticulating in their efforts to illustrate the manner of throwing the 'pelota' ball in real play was so unusual that it came nearer holding a quorum than have any of the fiery speeches that have been made for or against Gen. Wood's confirmation," reported the *Washington Post*.

The senators argued about the relationship between jai alai and gambling. Some said gambling was not essential to enjoying the sport; others said jai alai depended on betting privileges. Wood's opponents claimed by allowing the Jai Alai Fronton concession, he had saddled Havana for ten years with a "dreadful gambling establishment." Senators who attended the games in Havana testified that Basque jai alai coupled with gambling was an established and popular sporting tradition in Cuba. While controversial, the propriety of the game and Wood's conduct passed the Senate's scrutiny. Wood sailed for the Philippines at the end of March 1903. Rathbone lost; Wood won.

This was not to say jai alai, although well patronized, escaped criticism in Cuba. In 1904 Cuban senator Manuel Sanguily spoke before his colleagues. Jai alai was a "social cancer whose results are the moral and material ruin of many persons, the cause of commercial failures, and of the suicides of fathers of families and youths of brilliant promise." True, at least one well-known Havana gentleman committed suicide because he lost the family hacienda to his bookmaker. And in the stands bloody fistfights broke out between rival fans. Once, an overwrought bettor drew his pistol, cocked both barrels, and shouted, "You sold" (threw the game), while aiming his gun at the losing player. It seems a little bit of everything came with jai alai: traditionalism and commercialism, entertainment and risk.

Despite the criticism, by the end of Havana Jai Alai Fronton's ten-year contract, jai alai was more popular than bullfighting in Cuba. The city of Havana assumed control of the operation of the Jai Alai Fronton, known as The Palace of Screams (*El Palacio de los Gritos*), and new frontons for competition play opened throughout Cuba. Jai alai was a big-league sport, big-money business where emotions ran high in anticipation of losing or winning bets, coupled with the excitement of watching superb athletes. Fans, many of them adventure seekers from Miami, Florida, came for the magic of the game, the glamor of a nightclub, and the lure of gambling. Basque Ball impacted Cuba like a volcano, its eruption violent with "lava now made of jai alai," said author Antonio Méndez Muñiz. Jai alai "would forever burn itself into the minds and hearts of Cubans." So it seemed at the time.

It was also the time of freshly minted New York Yankees baseball player Babe Ruth. On October 29, 1920, Ruth arrived in Havana to play in an exhibition series with the New York Giants and the professional Habana and Almendares teams. As a celebrity attraction, he was paid two thousand dollars a game by his promoters. Ruth arrived late in Havana, almost two weeks after the series had begun, and stayed until November 11, skipping the last game because he demanded more money and was not given it. Still, the Cubans worshipped Ruth, and Ruth enjoyed Cuba. He played the horses at the Oriental Park Racetrack, and then could not resist the challenge, an extra challenge since he was left-handed, of learning to use the cesta. In a silk shirt and white flannel pants he practiced with the pros at the Havana fronton where he was a regular at the evening competitive matches. Reportedly, he lost most of his earnings, thousands of dollars, at the horse races and jai alai games.

The 1940s was the time of novelist Ernest Hemingway. Ten miles east of Havana at Finca Vigía (Lookout Farm), Hemingway made his home in Cuba. There in 1942 in the middle of World War II, he chased German U-boats off the coast. Hemingway devised his own operation, an adventure fit for a man of action. He planned to disable a one-thousand-ton U-boat and prevent it from submerging, creating an easy-to-track submarine for the United States military. Daily he and his "spy

Figure 4.2. Babe Ruth playing jai alai in Havana, Cuba, 1920s. Historic Postcard.

group" aboard the *Pilar*, a forty-foot fishing boat, patrolled the coast. They fished, planning to use fresh catch to lure the hungry crew of the U-boat. They hoped that the submarine would surface and its commander would ask for food. Then, the fishermen would throw a jury-rigged grenade into the narrow open hatch of the submarine. And who was better for the throw than a jai alai player? Thus, Francisco "Paxtchi" Ibarlucia, a Basque player at Havana Jai Alai, joined the crew. "When they call us alongside, the boys will clear the deck with the machine guns and Paxtchi will throw the bomb into the hatch," said Hemingway. Paxtchi never used his throwing arm. Submarine hunting in Cuba was a bust.

But every party has to come to an end. The revolutionary Fidel Castro arrived, and jai alai in Cuba died. On January 1, 1959, Castro led the overthrow of military dictator Fulgencio

Batista, setting the stage for the transformation to today's communist government. The new government broke from the past. "The previous sports organization had to be destroyed, the ruling anarchy eliminated, the existing flaws and vices eradicated," said author Rafael Cambo Arcos.

It is said that avid sportsman and all-around athlete Castro was a fan of jai alai and even played the game. It is also said that Castro's rebels took refuge in the vast Havana fronton to hide from Batista's troops. And that the firing squad of the Revolution lined up prisoners against the interior fronton walls and shot them, leaving behind imprints of bullet holes. It is said Cuban fans knew their jai alai as well as the Basques. No matter. There was no jai alai in life after the Cuban Revolution.

"The Palace of Screams," Havana, Cuba, 1957

In 1957 Basque backcourter Francisco Churruca signed to play the season at the Jai Alai Fronton in Havana. "If you didn't play well in Cuba, they didn't choose you to play in other places. Cuba was like a test," says Churruca. Churruca played very well. He actually ran up the sidewall, climbing maybe as high as ten feet to retrieve a difficult shot that stayed close to the wall. "I learned the hard way. One day I said to myself, I want to do that and put one foot on the wall, lunged and bang, hit my nose and face on the wall, and fell," he says. "The way to do it is get up as much speed as possible and push off the floor with one foot on the wall. With enough force I can climb a couple steps up the wall, catch the ball with my cesta, and throw the ball back before my feet hit the floor again. The beauty of the shot is getting back in position to return the next shot."

In 1958 Miami Jai Alai recruited Churruca. It was an opportunity up the professional ladder and he took it. Once he went back to Havana, it was a year later in 1959, and Fidel Castro was prime minister. Ironically, the fledgling regime turned to jai alai, the soon-to-be-chastised sport in the soon-to-be shut down Havana Jai Alai Fronton, when it needed money to replenish its chaotic treasury. It came to this, a jai alai tournament, a benefit performance to raise money for a charitable cause, the people of the Republic of Cuba. The Cubans remembered good times at jai alai.

The Cuban organizers invited a large number of competitors, the best in the region to attract the crowds. One of them from Miami was Churruca, known as the "Babe Ruth of Jai Alai." And in the end, he won the grand prize, a silver trophy.

"It was the first official trophy of the Revolution," says Churruca. "Castro wasn't there to see me win but his supporters were . . . like Che Guevara."

"Would you like to have Castro's signature engraved on the trophy?" said Castro's personal assistant.

"Sure. Because Castro was a big deal and this man promised to return the trophy before I left Havana to go back to Miami."

Churruca handed him his trophy. "And I never saw it again."

In 1962, the revolutionary Republic of Cuba outlawed jai alai as a professional sport with its attendant commercialism and gambling. Private investors controlled jai alai for their economic gain, contract bosses limited opportunity for the masses, and betting corrupted, so went the political philosophy. Abruptly, the matches ended and frontons closed. The Palace of Screams was quiet. The players followed the next path of opportunity across the Florida Straits to the United States, where jai alai took on a life of its own.

5
THE QUESTION OF GAMBLING

At the beginning of April 1904 in Havana, Cuba, twelve jai alai players and their manager, on loan from the famous Havana Jai Alai, boarded a steamship on the Southern Pacific Atlantic Steamship Line bound for New Orleans, Louisiana. There in New Orleans they transferred to the steamer *Louisiana* and sailed the inland waterway of the Mississippi River to St. Louis, Missouri, in time to entertain visitors to the World's Fair with jai alai.

On April 30, David Francis, president of the Louisiana Purchase Exposition, pounded a granite historical maker into the ground, and said, "Open ye gates. Swing wide, ye portals." About two hundred thousand people passed through the gates on opening day of the Louisiana Purchase Centennial Exposition, popularly called the World's Fair. For the next seven months until the fair closed on December 1, an estimated twenty million people celebrated progress with the latest technological innovations in science and achievements in the arts. From the nearly three-hundred-foot DeForest Wireless Telegraph Tower, visitors sent wireless messages, as astonishing as an early cellular phone. Along the mile-long arcade, "The Pike," fairgoers rode a camel at Hagenbeck's Zoological Paradise and Animal Circus and swayed 265 feet above the ground on top of the Great Observation Wheel. Sports enthusiasts, drawn to the St. Louis Summer Olympic Games, the first held in the United States, would discover another sport—jai alai. Or so the jai alai promoters hoped.

At the corner of DeBaliviere Avenue and Kingsbury Place, near the main entrance of the World's Fair, the Cuban Jai Alai Company inaugurated the first commercial jai alai fronton in the United States. Plans began in 1903 when a group of investors inspired by the success of jai alai in Cuba organized the Cuban Jai Alai Company, licensed in Missouri. Three of the company officers—President Ricardo Gabis Ajuria, also president of the National Bank of Spain in Cuba; Vice President F. M. Steinhart, treasurer of the Bank of Spain; and Secretary C. Quintero Lamar, United States consul to Cuba—were from Havana. The other two officers—B. Zarasquota, second vice president, and Vice Secretary Charles Ledden—lived in St. Louis. These were the entrepreneurs who introduced jai alai at the World's Fair as an entertaining spectator sport. They predicted enthusiastic Missouri fans would pressure their lawmakers to legalize jai alai as a gambling sport. Given their experience in Cuba, betting attracted the attention and money of the casual sports patron. Without betting, jai alai's cultural and social significance as a sport in the Basque Country was irrelevant in the heartland of America.

So this was jai alai as a commodity. But Ricardo Gabis, the company president, also had a personal interest in the St. Louis Fronton. He built the building. Gabris was a native Spaniard, educated in the mid-1800s at the University of Madrid as a civil engineer. He wandered, first to Puerto Rico where he undertook the construction of the canal of San Juan Harbor, and then to Havana where he lent his expertise to the first railroad system in Cuba. There in Havana he pursued his instinct for business and became the president of the Banco Español de la Isla de Cuba (Bank of Spain in Cuba). He followed his passion for jai alai and designed Havana Jai Alai, the "Palace of Screams," and he married. Gabris was a solid Havana citizen—until he disagreed with the brutal policies of the Spanish military governor general Valeriano Weyler and in self-imposed exile moved to the United States in 1896. Yet Gabris did not forget about jai alai.

In St. Louis, Gabris designed the jai alai fronton to be similar to Havana Jai Alai. "An interior court, 210 feet long and 36 feet wide, is being provided for the game of pelota, the national game of Spain, and walls, 16 feet high, of Missouri granite, are being built at either end of the court," announced the *St. Louis Daily Globe-Democrat* on January 31, 1904. Most of the buildings erected at the World's Fair were temporary structures framed in wood and covered with a mixture of plaster of paris and hemp fibers called "staff." Not so the jai alai fronton. At an estimated cost of $250,000 with a seating capacity of thousands, the building was built to last with a steel-fabricated interior and an exterior of brick, stone, terracotta, and iron.

On Sunday, May 15, 1904, St. Louis played jai alai. Hawkers hired by the Cuban Jai Alai Company dispersed throughout the World's Fair exhibition grounds, pressing flyers into the hands of fairgoers. They shouted, "Inaugural game, 3:00 p.m.; miss it, catch the 8:30 evening game." They boasted about the "most interesting, scientific, exciting, greatest ball game in the world."

But jai alai in St. Louis did not catch on as a spectator sport. Play by play, the announcer at the games explained what was happening on the court. Even so, the audience felt jai alai was a foreign experience with players they did not recognize and whose names they could not pronounce, and tactics they could not understand. Added to that, they had no opportunity to test their luck betting on the outcome of the matches in anti-gambling Missouri. No doubt the sport was a show of speed and skill, but the public's enthusiasm was short-lived. Two months after St. Louis Jai Alai opened, it closed.

"It was hoped that the game would become popular in St. Louis, and then spread to Chicago, New York, New Orleans and San Francisco," reported the *St. Louis Daily Globe-Democrat*. But jai alai in St. Louis was a financial and sports failure. The officers dissolved the Cuban Jai Alai Company, and Gabris returned home to Havana, where he resumed his previous position as president of the Bank of Spain.

The meticulously constructed building once used to play jai alai survived. Long after St. Louisans forgot jai alai they remembered roller-skating and ice-skating at the converted fronton, renamed the Winter Garden. In 1964 the landmark building was demolished, replaced by a shopping center.

●

The World's Fair venture was not the first attempt to bring professional jai alai to the United States. Two years earlier on January 10, 1902, among the weekly sales listed "In the Real Estate Field" of the *New York Times* was a block front of Central Park West properties. "That a Havana syndicate stood ready to handle a million-dollar real estate and building operation in this city, hoping for success in the popularity of the Spanish game of pelota, caused a look of astonishment on the faces of many, but such is the fact, according to the New York representative of the Havana company, and within two or three years it is predicted that pelota will have supplanted golf, football, hockey, and half a dozen other pastimes in the hearts of New Yorkers," reported the *Times*. New Yorkers heard nothing more about the project. It was a case of economics. Without the excitement of heavy betting and the subsequent revenue of gambling, jai alai as a professional sport was a risk the "Havana syndicate," a group of silent partners, apparently were not prepared to undertake.

Up to that point, Basque immigrants in the western part of the United States played their Basque Ball as recreation and a cultural tradition. With the discovery of gold in California in 1848, large numbers of Basque from the "settler societies" of Argentina, Chile, Brazil, and Uruguay joined the rush to mine gold, then silver, in the American West. Others recognized opportunity in vast farmland and open-range livestock districts, and Basque ranchers and sheepherders migrated to California, Nevada, Oregon, and Idaho.

In the American West, the Basque boardinghouse, *ostatua*, became the social and cultural center for the Basque immigrant community. Usually, the immigrant connection originated in New York City, where weary Basque travelers passed through Ellis Island and embarked from passenger ships docked in the busy Manhattan harbor. "Euskaldunak emen badira (Are there any Basques here)," shouted hotelkeepers like Valentin Aguirre, one of their own from Spanish Viscaya. "One can certainly imagine the overwhelming relief the Basques felt," writes historian Gloria Totoricagüena.

At 82 Bank Street in Greenwich Village, thousands of the new Basque immigrants recovered from their ocean voyage at Valentin and Benita Aguirre's transit hotel, the Santa Lucia (also named Casa Vizainĩa). There they traded stories over a familiar lunch of *sopa de ajo con huevos* (garlic soup with eggs) at the Jai Alai Restaurant and Bar. In lieu of the traditional handball court, the "Jai Alai" was a piece of home. Next door, Aguirre ran a travel agency where the westward-bound Basque bought train tickets to continue their journey on the Transcontinental Railroad.

In Boise, Idaho, the typical young male sheepherder stopped where he found work in the high mountain pastures and booked room and board at a Basque-owned boardinghouse. When he was not living for long isolated periods of time in charge of flocks of sheep on open range, the boarding house was his "home away from home." There he slept in a clean room, ate traditional Basque food, prospected for jobs, met girlfriends, and played Basque handball.

Juan and Juana Anduiza's hotel on Grove Street in Boise offered a special amenity. Instead of a boardinghouse with the usual adjacent outdoor two-walled ball court, the long handball court named the "Anduiza Fronton" was in the hotel basement. A few small windows ran along the top of the ceiling. The space was large, more than 150 feet, ideal for dance parties and potluck dinners sponsored by the Boise immigrants. But at every opportunity the men reserved the court to play their native ball game, either for fun or tournament play. Between friends and friends of friends they bet "cash money," sometimes as heavy as five to ten thousand dollars for a match.

The boardinghouse Basques played the traditional handball game with their bare hands. "Local players used to play until their hands swelled up. At that point, they'd enlist the help of the boardinghouse owner 'Big Jack' Anduiza, who would press their hands under a board, then stand on the board to reduce the swelling," said one elderly Boise Basque to historian Mark Bieter.

At times, the players switched to a homemade paddle or bat, but rarely the cesta of jai alai fame. For this was the early 1900s in the rural American West. There were no national jai alai organizations with lucrative competitive matches to attract experienced players. The large indoor jai alai frontons with exacting court specifications took up a lot of space, and construction costs ran high. The wicker cesta, a specialized piece of throwing and catching equipment, was expensive and scarce, handcrafted from Basque native materials by traditional master cesta-makers. The cesta required a skill to construct and a learning curve to catch and throw, whereas most every child in the Basque Country knew how to play Basque handball, sometimes competing with as many as forty children in a round-robin game on the village plaza. "Handball is a people's game, all you need is a wall and a ball," says historian David Lachiondo.

Eventually, governmental regulations of public domain lands and immigration quotas affected Basque settlement. By the end of the 1930s, the era of the Basque sheepherder and rancher in the American West had pretty well passed, taking with it the Basque boardinghouses and attendant Basque Ball games. By then, the Basque sport of jai alai had traveled a different route, arriving as spectator entertainment in Miami, Florida, on the crest of the Florida Land Boom.

●

In the 1920s, Southern Florida boomed. "The millions of

drained acres (with plenty millions more still underwater) lay waiting for the spark to ignite get-rich-quick dreaming," writes author Herb Hiller. In 1924 on a remote piece of filled-in swampland in Hialeah Park, ten lonely miles from Miami, three investors from Cuba acted on an opportunity to bring professional jai alai to Florida. They constructed a plain, shed-like building on the site of the present-day parking lot of Hialeah Park Racing and Casino and named it Biscayne Jai Alai, later known as Miami Jai Alai. It was here at Hialeah Park that the Miami Kennel Club raced greyhounds and the Miami Jockey Club raced thoroughbreds. The most curious of the sporting crowd ventured outside the racing grandstand to the nearby jai alai fronton where they watched a roster of up-and-coming Spanish players imported from Cuba compete against each other in the new Florida winter sport.

The promoters introduced jai alai as a professional sport at Hialeah, but it was not a legal gambling event—even though Florida had a history of gambling, vacillating from societal acceptance to resistance, from government prohibition to regulation. Even Presbyterian business tycoon Henry Flagler in the latter part of the 1880s enticed affluent winter visitors to his grand Ponce de Leon Hotel in St. Augustine with the thrill of illicit gambling. Here on the Atlantic Coast at the Ponce's exclusive Bacchus Club, the elite lost or won at roulette wheels, craps tables, or bookie boards. Meanwhile on the Gulf Coast in Tampa, the working class played the illegal numbers game *bolita*, a type of lottery imported from Cuba.

By the mid-1920s crowds packed the stands of Hialeah Park Racetrack to enjoy the traditional betting sport of horse racing, even though organized gambling was illegal. But cash-laden winter tourists and risk-taking locals were unhappy;

Figure 5.1. Jai Alai Fronton—Hialeah, Florida, 1924. Courtesy of W. A. Fishbaugh, State Archives of Florida, Florida Memory, Tallahassee, Florida.

they wanted to go to the races and bet. Racetrack operators wanted to satisfy the customers.

As the would-be gamblers were undeterred, bold and resourceful wagering went on at Hialeah during various time periods in various versions, under the interpretation that betting was not the same as gambling if it was not connected to organized bookmakers. In the 1890s in New York thoroughbred horse racing fans had turned to the marginally legal oral betting system to circumvent the law against racetrack gambling. No odds posted, no open passing of money, no recording of bets (though the serious bettor could find a bookmaker circulating among the crowd). Under the guise of private betting, this early method was good enough for New Yorkers.

Or racetrack patrons placed their bets through the medium of picture postcards, also referred to as the stock certificate option. The bettor bought a postcard of an individual horse entered in the race. If the horse won, the track bought back the postcard and paid to the buyer a dividend that coincided with the winning odds. If the horse lost, the postcard was worthless, and the bettor collected nothing.

It was here at Hialeah that the budding Miami Jai Alai conducted its games in the shadow of racing's betting schemes. Betting on an outstanding jai alai player was like betting on a champion horse. Legally, no open betting was allowed, but in reality, spectators exchanged money—more than a few friendly bets took place.

Jai alai's tenure as the Hialeah Racetrack's next-door neighbor was short-lived. On September 18, 1926, the Cape Verde Islands–born hurricane, called the Great Miami Hurricane, or the Big Blow, struck Miami as a Category 4, the second highest classification on the Saffir-Simpson Hurricane Scale. What that meant for coastal residents of South Florida was maximum sustained winds of 130–150 mph, 12–15-feet storm surges, rainfall-induced floods, catastrophic property damage in the millions, and the loss of more than one hundred lives. Most people were asleep when the sole South Florida radio station broadcast the 11:00 p.m. hurricane warning. According to observations gathered by today's National Hurricane Center, Richard Gray, at the time head of the National Weather Service Bureau in Miami, ran through the dark streets of Miami to warn people. Later, in the early hours of morning after the eye of the hurricane passed, Gray returned to the streets, this time to shout that the storm was not over. "The worst is yet to come!" The worst came, for this was the typical lull before the winds swept from the opposite direction with greater force than before on the young city of Miami. The hurricane left Hialeah Park in ruins, a sign, said anti-gambling believers, of "a just retribution by God!"

The hastily erected jai alai building at Hialeah did not stand much of a chance to survive the Great Miami Hurricane. Winds tore off the roof, rains flooded the interior, and the walls collapsed. Less than two years old, the Hialeah fronton was leveled, an opportunity seized by a group of investors, this time from Boston, Massachusetts, to relocate and revitalize jai alai in Miami.

One day in Boston Richard I. Berenson met with the governing officers of the Fronton Exhibition Company Inc., owner of "Miami Jai-A-Lai," established at its present location near the Miami International Airport. They talked business. Miami Jai-A-Lai was losing money, and Berenson turned around struggling businesses. Thus it was that Berenson, a northeasterner from Boston, moved south to Miami to become general manager of Miami Jai Alai with a 10 percent company stock incentive.

Fixing a broken jai alai business turned out to be successful for Berenson and his associates but it was far from easy or quick. Berenson dealt with expenses, revenues, and operations, ongoing activities related to the core of the business. He looked at cash-in and cash-out. There was no cash-in from wagering, because gambling on a jai alai player was illegal. But apparently there was some cash-out, which went to "unsavory outside people" who installed slot machines inside the building and set the odds against hitting a winning combination, driving away angry jai alai customers. "My grandfather was tough and fearless," says Berenson's grandson, Richard B. Berenson. "With the help of a security guard, he ripped out and dragged the rigged slot machines into the street. He called the local sheriff and said, 'No deal anymore. Come and get the slot machines; they're out in front along the street.'"

Berenson had a vision for jai alai. What did Miamians and winter visitors want from a night out in the tropical playground of Miami? "When the half-million-dollar Biscayne fronton on N. W. 36th St. throws open its doors . . . the beautiful fronton will be a blaze of lights," said the *Miami Daily News* on the upcoming opening night of the season in 1929. "Free dancing for patrons will also be one of the attractions this season, and with Marie Kerkhol's society orchestra, formerly of the Everglades, furnishing the music, many delightful dance parties are anticipated." Soon the glassed nightclub on the fifth floor of the top of the modern fronton—built to stand solid in a hurricane—became an added attraction.

What did sports fans expect? "Sterling players engage in their nightly duels with the cesta and bullet-like ball," said the *Miami Daily News*. Berenson gave the fans what they wanted: fast action in a thrilling tactical game played by skilled players recruited from the best of the teams in Europe and Latin America.

Still, people wanted to bet. They wagered for fun and to make money. In 1931 amid controversy and almost over Governor Doyle Carlton's dead body, Florida legalized pari-mutuel gambling for horse and dog racing.

Governor Carlton crusaded against gambling. In 1929 Carlton targeted Hialeah Race Park, the three greyhound racing tracks, the Miami (Biscayne) jai alai fronton—and Al Capone. "Florida was not a haven for crooks and criminals nor the headquarters for gangsters and gunmen," said Carlton. Particularly Capone, the notorious organized crime boss from

Figure 5.2. Biscayne Jai Alai Fronton Miami, Florida, 1926. Courtesy of State Archives of Florida, Florida Memory, Tallahassee, Florida.

Chicago, was not welcome in Florida as a winter resident. He was "a menace to the safety and well-being of residents."

On March 20, 1930, Carlton telegrammed the sheriffs in Florida. "It is reported that Al Capone is on his way to Florida. Arrest promptly if he comes your way and escort him to State borders with instructions not to return. He cannot remain in Florida. If you need additional assistance, call me." This appeared to be an illegal method to hassle Capone, but an officer followed orders and arrested Capone when he crossed the state line into Florida. After spending a few hours in the local jail, Capone was released and continued south to Miami, where he made his home until he died in 1947. Carlton did not get rid of Capone or gambling.

It was the beginning of the 1930s. Florida faced financial problems. Its cities and the state were in debt. It was a time when the United States stock market crashed, the Great Depression devastated both rich and poor, and the Florida real estate boom collapsed. The Great Miami Hurricane in 1926 and the 1928 Okeechobee Hurricane damaged land and cities. In 1929 the Mediterranean fruit fly decimated the citrus crop. As spirits and the economy sank, proponents of legalized betting argued that gambling brought in tax revenue. Gambling operated in spite of prohibition, so it was better to regulate what was difficult to stop.

Governor Carlton made enemies. He cut state salaries and eliminated jobs to balance the budget, but most notably he created controversy when he opposed the state getting into the gambling business. On August 17, 1930, in Jacksonville, Florida, the sheriff jailed three men accused of conspiracy to "bump off the governor." Were the accused trying to stop the governor from limiting gambling? Was Capone involved? The case was dismissed.

In May 1931, Carlton vetoed the proposed pari-mutuel race bill that came before the Florida legislature. "It is unsound and unwise from an economic, political, or moral standpoint to commit the state to a partnership in legalized gambling in any form. If we start with pari-mutuels, where shall we stop?" Carlton said.

Did he come "unhitched," asked members of the Palm Beach winter horse racing set? "If the state doesn't give me a pari-mutuel law I will abandon the plant (Hialeah) to the weeds and the people to their fate," said Joseph Widener, owner of the Hialeah Racetrack, to the *Chicago Tribune*.

Then on June 5, 1931, the Florida legislature overrode Carlton's veto by one switched vote. Florida legalized pari-mutuel gambling at the horse and dog racetracks, regulated, governed, and supervised by a five-member State Racing Commission. The state received a 3 percent tax on pari-mutuel wagering and a 15 percent tax on the admission fee earmarked for equal distribution to Florida's sixty-seven counties.

True to his promise, Joseph Widener invested millions of dollars to transform Hialeah Racetrack into one of the world's most outstanding racecourses. On January 18, 1933, Widener said, "Florida racing will have its greatest year." It was undeniable that racing crowds craved the extra excitement of gambling.

The question for nearby Miami Jai Alai was how to get the sport of jai alai added to the list of Florida's legalized pari-mutuel activities. As the novelty of the sport wore off, Miami Jai Alai struggled to survive and establish a stable legal and financial base. "Without the gambling legislation, the fronton will close next year," said Berenson.

The question of gambling opened and closed other jai alai frontons in other places. On December 21, 1927, in Chicago, Illinois, Mayor William Thompson and prominent Chicago citizens turned out in large numbers for opening night of the new indoor winter entertainment, professional jai alai at the Rainbo Gardens Fronton. "Chicago's brand of jai alai looks like the real thing. Expect wagering to add zest to games," said columnist "Mexican Joe." But in this city called "gambling crazy," no gambling was permitted at the jai alai games, an attempt by the state attorney of Cook County to crack down on mobsters involved in gambling. Even so, the jai alai spectators bet individually among each other, or bet the curious Allen Purse System, contributing to a winner's prize, the "purse." For a time, Chicagoans filled the fronton and newspapers published game scores and players' profiles, but skill was not the main factor of popularity. Most fans picked their favorites by a player's shirt color or pronounceable name. They needed the challenge of wagering to allow them to engage in the game, but gambling on jai alai did not happen, and the fronton was eventually converted to a wrestling and boxing arena.

Meanwhile, in Shanghai, China, the betting sport of jai alai, known as "hai alai," prospered. In 1930 a roster of mainly Basque jai alai players competed on the court of the modernist Art Deco fronton, the Hai Alai Auditorium. In the years that followed, the stock company inspired by Basque entrepreneur Teodoro Jaureqi added a splendid circular bar and expanded the seating capacity to three thousand. Some of the sport's most famous players competed in singles and doubles, as many as sixteen matches a day. The house, the Hai Alai Company, prospered by withholding 15–20 percent of each bet. Unlucky Shanghainese bettors pronounced the game "hai'a'la," a wordplay that implied "to entrap and make poor." Yet attendance and vigorous betting flourished, fanned by the pleasure of the Chinese who historically gambled at the horse races and on the games of fan-tan and *pai gow*. Then came the 1949 Communist Revolution and the People's Republic of China and Chairman Mao Zedong (Mao Tse-tung). Mao initiated a massive crack-down against gambling, which he considered a symbol of capitalist corruption. With that change in the business climate, Shanghai Hai Alai closed.

It was obvious that wagering held the interest of the typical spectator of jai alai. "There are, when all's said and done, only a handful of spectator sports which make the general public's blood, and the gate receipts, flow like sap in the springtime," said journalist John Lardner. "Baseball." Lardner grew up with three long-time popular sports in the United States: baseball, basketball, and football. What did it take for jai alai to break through? Berenson continued to press for pari-mutuel wagering at Miami Jai Alai.

In 1934 Berenson scarcely thought twice about tackling the challenge of lobbying Governor David Sholtz and the Florida legislators, one by one, to permit gambling as a legal betting event at Miami Jai Alai. Berenson pointed out that in 1931, the first year of legalized pari-mutuel wagering at the three horse tracks and six dog tracks, the state raised over $737,000 in revenue from a pari-mutuel source of over seventeen million dollars. He noted in 1931 the racing industry increased jobs, employing about seven thousand people, a reference to the pledge of Governor Sholtz, elected in 1933 during the Great Depression, to get his constituents back to work. Berenson and his supporters finally succeeded. The legislature coupled jai alai with pari-mutuel racing, enabling jai alai to follow the path of mainstream gambling sports.

On July 20, 1935, the commissioners of the Florida State Racing Commission granted a permit to the Fronton Exhibition Company Inc. to operate the gambling sport of jai alai at Miami Jai-A-Lai in Dade County. "The city fathers of Miami ought to erect a plaque at Northwest 36th Street and Douglas Avenue to commemorate a historic event that has influenced modern life. It might read: 'Exotic Track Wagering Was Invented Here by Richard I. Berenson,'" says journalist Andrew Beyer.

Miami Jai Alai was back on its feet with a new level of interest and credibility with the public.

6
THE RISE OF JAI ALAI

Good things happened to jai alai in Florida. Jai alai was a hit with sports enthusiasts who enjoyed the athletic spectacle, especially with a pari-mutuel ticket in their hand. The men liked it because the speed and force of the ball were inherently dangerous. It was a "man's game," said Mexican revolutionary Pancho Villa. The women said the players looked like foreign movie idols.

Jai alai in Florida was more than an exciting fast-paced spectator sport branded as an exotic import. It was a sports industry that brought in money and contributed to the economy. Within a year after the 1935 legalization of jai alai as a pari-mutuel sport, the game's revenue proved to be a substantial source of income for the fronton shareholders and the state. To promoters of Miami Jai Alai, the sport's debut in New York seemed a logical progression. Surely, what worked in Florida would work in New York, where loyal sports fans filled the stands of boxing matches, baseball games, and horse races. And thousands of New Yorkers already attended a night or two at the jai alai games while vacationing in Florida during the winter, and many of them were bettors. In 1938, New York boxing promoter Mike Jacobs and theater producer Levi "Lee" Shubert collaborated with Miami Jai Alai's Richard Berenson to bring jai alai to New Yorkers.

On Thursday, September 8, 1938, Segundo, Piston, Guillermo, and Gabriel, the star "Four Aces" from Cuba, played the premier opening night match on the court at the jai alai fronton constructed in the entire east quadrant of the 240-foot-long old Hippodrome Theater in Manhattan. It was a most unusual venue for a jai alai fronton.

In 1905 New York showmen Frederick Thompson and Elmer Dundy, partners in Luna Park amusements at Coney Island, built the block-long grand theater at Sixth Avenue in Manhattan. They named it the Hippodrome after the European indoor circus theaters. The New York Hippodrome was "a palace . . . a building to rouse wonder and eagerness," says author Norman Clarke. Designed by architect J. H. Morgan, ornate Arabesque towers lit with electric globes topped the corners of the multistory brick building. On a stage twelve times larger than any on Broadway, as many as a thousand actors, singers, and dancers captured the imagination of a capacity crowd of 5,200 people with four-hour extravagances, complete with circus horses, and elephants and tigers. Swimmers and divers performed water ballets in an eight-thousand-gallon glass water tank that rose from below the stage by hydraulic pistons.

Tastes and costs and owners changed. Vaudeville and movies replaced lavish shows at the Hippodrome. In 1918 illusionist Harry Houdini staged the disappearance of the ten-thousand-pound "vanishing elephant." In 1919 movie goers watched the first-run silent movie *Better Times* directed by King Vidor. After that, the Hippodrome declined into a

Figure 6.1. Jai Alai at the Hippodrome, New York, New York, 1938. Poster Front View. Courtesy of Jim Liversidge Collection, Special and Area Studies Collections, George A. Smathers Libraries, University of Florida, Gainesville, Florida.

sad semblance of its former glory, reduced to budget performances of plays, operas, and discount movies. By 1938 the facility had downsized to a sports arena for boxing and wrestling events. So it was, jai alai starred at the Hippodrome.

"The most beautiful opening you ever saw, a beautiful show. Marie Gravere sang a hymn of jai alai. Mr. Berenson gave a talk, and it was the first time they were going to have radio coverage from coast to coast . . . There were three hundred writers from all over the world to cover it and everyone was dressed in tuxedos and women in long dresses—beautiful," said Miami player-manager Pedro Mir.

Berenson tapped his creative resources to catch the fancy of the New York crowd. Ushers dressed as matadors, and

Figure 6.2. Jai Alai at the Hippodrome, New York, New York, 1938. Poster Back View. Courtesy of Jim Liversidge Collection, Special and Area Studies Collections, George A. Smathers Libraries, University of Florida, Gainesville, Florida.

attendants wore berets and Spanish Andalusian-style short, cropped jackets. Sometimes between games volunteers from the audience stepped on court, strapped a cesta on one hand, and threw the ball. That was when wild shots broke the glass on the scoreboard. "Americans are becoming more enthused about the sport. They're even learning Spanish cheers and curses," said the *New York Sun*.

The *New Yorker* disagreed. "The night jai alai opened at the Hippodrome an announcer in a wire cage told the audience how to behave. When there was a good shot, he asked for applause; when somebody made an error, he called for hisses & boos. When the teams were tied at the last point he said it was customary for everyone to stand up and yell. This attempt to impose Mediterranean fervor didn't seem to work out very well. George Jean Nathan indignantly put on his hat and went home. We're afraid Mike Jacobs is going to have a hard time making New Yorkers act like Basques, especially on top of a heavy meal, and we're sure the Hippodrome is the wrong place to try it."

Initially, the game attracted followers. "Jai alai, the world's fastest game, which has clicked with the world's fastest town, marked the hundredth performance at the New York Hippodrome last night," reported the *New York Sun* on November 22, 1938. But attendance slumped. "There's no interest in jai alai around here," said Jacobs.

It was true that the general public, who grew up playing baseball and basketball instead of jai alai, did not fully understand the tactics of the game. But Jacobs and Shubert based the success of their venture on betting interest. They intended to convince the New York powers that be that the sport was clean, the players honest, and legalized gambling a financial asset to the state. Yet the New York Gaming Commission said "no" to jai alai as a gambling sport. Now the primary economic gain for the venture had to come from admission sales. Not enough, the investors said, and cut their losses. Jai alai at the Hippodrome closed in the spring after one short season. The jai alai players returned to their home courts, some to Cuba, Mexico, and Spain, and others to Florida. Berenson returned to his office above the court at the Miami Fronton.

Miami Jai Alai continued to thrive, even during the course of World War II. Miami and surrounding Dade County—with its warm climate, level land, and proximity to the waterways and ocean—proved ideal for military bases, aviation operations, and training facilities. At the Port of

Miami the United States Navy trained submariners, the "Donald Duck Navy," to live and work underwater for a long time in their autonomous warship home. The Army Air Force Transport Command claimed the Miami Municipal Airport. Overflow military personnel bunked in motels and hotels, some beachside at the Hollywood Beach Hotel, others at the elegant Biltmore Hotel in Coral Gables. Civilian men and women worked double shifts to build ships and weld metal airplane parts. Even the regional citrus farmers thrived, growing oranges for the innovative process of frozen concentrated orange juice, and controlling insects with the pesticide DDT (dichlorodiphenyltrichloroethane), now banned. Miami, named the Magic City in the 1920s because of its unprecedented growth, surged in population during the war years from 173,000 to 300,000.

After hours, job done, soldiers, sailors, Marines, airmen, nurses, factory workers, and local businesspeople sought entertainment. They found it at Miami Jai Alai. Here, they escaped from a hard day's work, had a bite to eat, bet a few dollars, and jeered and cheered. For members of a troop scheduled for overseas deployment, the fast-paced action game offered a temporary diversion. For tourists, those who took to heart the slogan "Like a Soldier YOU Need a Civilian Furlough," the jai alai game program was a souvenir of a Miami holiday. However, the United States was mobilized for war, and most people did not have the time or inclination to travel for pleasure.

Postwar South Florida continued to outshine the rest of the Sunbelt. Pan Am Field merged with the Army Air Transport Field to form the Miami International Airport. Former military personnel who were stationed in Miami returned to live or vacation there. In 1946 President Harry Truman joined the snowbirds and settled in at the "Little White House" in Key West, a scenic trip down the Overseas Highway from Miami. The economy was strong and people were optimistic and tourists returned. Miami was the "playground of the world and one of the most delightful cities in the world in which to live permanently." Swim, boat, fish, golf, watch football at the Orange Bowl, and bet on the horses at the Hialeah Racetrack or the players at the jai alai fronton. This was the time when Miami Jai Alai was the only professional fronton in the United States. Judged by breakthrough attendance records, one of the favorite things to do and see in Miami was jai alai.

"Jai alai players were treated by segments of Miamians and visitors as celebrities. In quest of a handshake and autograph, fans even followed them to the popular San Juan restaurant on S. W. 8th Street in today's Little Havana, where many players dined after games. These Basque natives were a tight-knit group who lived and dined together and were courteous to their supplicants. The players held a strong attraction to their fandom because of their athleticism, fearlessness, and good cheer," says historian Paul George, a native Miamian.

Jai alai succeeded in Miami, born from reclaimed Everglades swampland and transformed into "land by the gallon," as a gambling sport. Perhaps there was "the affinity between gambling and frontiers . . . From the seventeenth century through the twentieth, both gambling and westering thrived on high expectations, risk taking, opportunism, and movement," suggests historian John Findlay. In Florida with a long history of gambling, legal and illegal, there were those who enjoyed betting and welcomed pari-mutuel jai alai as harmless entertainment. Yet there were those who blamed

Figure 6.3. Group Portrait of Jai Alai Players at the Coral Gables Country Club, 1925. Courtesy of W. A. Fishbaugh, State Archives of Florida, Florida Memory, Tallahassee, Florida.

gambling for the ills of South Florida, reputed to be wide open for crime syndicates and corrupted pubic officials.

In 1941, the residents of Miami Beach, a coastal resort city separated from Miami by Biscayne Bay, said, "not in my backyard" to jai alai. State Senator Dewey Johnson of Brookville, Florida, had proposed Bill Number 753 to permit the construction of a jai alai fronton in Miami Beach. "A great many of us feel that the building of a jai alai fronton on Miami Beach would be a very desirable addition to our facilities for entertainment," said the president of the Venetian Islands Improvement Association of Miami Beach. The president of Artcraft Developmental Company, however, said, "We are of the firm belief that this type of thriller and its accompanying gambling feature are undesirable and against the best interest of the community." The bill failed, and there was no jai alai in Miami Beach.

Despite such objections, slowly but steadily the Basque sport of physical skill, strategy, and chance caught on, growing as Florida grew, spurred by exposure and a grassroots fan base. "My interest in jai alai began during my parents' annual escape from the cold of a New Jersey winter to the promised land of Florida. They stuffed the kids into a Ford station and drove a thousand miles in two days each way . . . The biggest draw came to be the one night each trip when we went to a fronton, or jai alai stadium, and watched them play," says computer scientist Steven Skiena. "In seven years, it'll eclipse baseball," pitched a jai alai investor to Manhattan advertising executive Don Draper in the retro-1960s television series *Mad Men*. It did not. Still, by 1974 jai alai had expanded to nine frontons, then ten, in Florida.

New and experienced entrepreneurs opened frontons with optimism in other states as well. In 1974 movie, automobile, and resort investor Kirk Kerkorian presented jai alai as part of the entertainment package at the MGM Grand Hotel in Las Vegas, Nevada. The curious ventured from the casino to the fronton built at the far end of the hotel, and walked back through the casino when they left the games. Four years later in Reno, Kerkorian opened his second MGM Grand Hotel and included jai alai as a betting option for his casino customers. 1976 and '77 were the years Connecticut and Rhode Island legalized pari-mutuel jai alai. State legislators realized it was "a kind of goose, which can lay golden pelotas which can readily be converted into schools, highways, and assorted state services," said author Katherine Hines Herrington.

And so young jai alai players turning professional in the 1950s, such as José Ramón Eizaguirre, lived the life of a traveling jai alai player. "Extremely good moments," he says.

Along the way his path crossed different time periods and chapters of global jai alai. From 1956 to 1983, first as a player, then players' manager, and later, referee, he played the international circuit—Spain, Mexico, and in the United States, Florida, Connecticut, and Nevada. In 1959 he almost played in Havana, Cuba, but revolutionary leader Fidel Castro banned gambling, and so all the frontons closed.

Eizaguirre was born in 1937 in the small rural town of Berriatura, Spain, in the low mountain valleys of the northern Basque County. He was three years old when he picked up a rubber handball and hit it again and again against the stone wall of his house. Most of every day of his childhood he played the wall and ball game, fortuitous preparation for the hand and eye coordination necessary for jai alai. "I learned on my own," he says. More than seventy years later, animated, light on his feet, Eizaguirre scooped up an imaginary ball with his treasured cesta and swung the cesta across his chest to demonstrate a backhand shot, this time in his townhouse kitchen in Windsor, Connecticut, instead on court before thousands of screaming fans. "He was a top frontcourt player," says professional jai alai player José Goitia.

When Eizaguirre was sixteen years old he signed his first professional contract with Las Palmas Fronton in the Spanish Canary Islands. Within three years he earned a positon on the roster at Tampa Jai Alai on the Gulf Coast of Florida. But Eizaguirre played a different style of jai alai in Spain than in the United States.

In Spain Eizaguirre played the long partido game, two players against two in a doubles match. He and his partner played until the team with the most stamina, strategy, and a bit of luck scored a preset amount of winning points up to thirty or thirty-five, occasionally forty, points. "I'm going to

Figure 6.4. José Eizaguirre Accepting Player's Trophy from Marlene Schmidt, Miss Universe, 1961. Courtesy of José Eizaguirre.

tell you the worst moment in my life as a player," says Eizaguirre. "It was in Durango, Spain, during the summer games. My partner was Churruca, one of the greatest backcourt players. Churruca dropped back and threw the ball to me, coming very easy. The thought passed through my mind; the only thing I have to do now to miss this easy catch is drop the ball. And I did. I hit the ball on the rim of my cesta. I wanted to disappear." The fans rushed to change their bets. For this was the Spanish bookmaker system: a point scored, odds changed, and the bettors increased or hedged their wagers, slipping their money inside a slit tennis ball and throwing it to one of the betting cashiers posted throughout the audience. On court the game ball bounced furious against the wall; in the packed stands the betting balls flew above heads.

In Florida Eizaguirre adjusted his play to the quiniela game, round-robin matches, fast-paced and quick-change. Eight rotating players took turns competing against each other until one team reached seven points. When Eizaguirre and his partner won the point, they stayed on court to meet the next team in rotation. When they lost, they left the court and went to the end of the line to wait their next turn to play. One doubles game: twelve to fifteen minutes. Eleven round-robin games: eleven different betting pools. For in Florida jai alai was the basis for pari-mutuel wagering: people won money from a pool of other people's money. No surprise, fronton shareholders and state legislators and bettors embraced the heightened drama and wagers of round-robin rotations.

By the 1967–1968 winter season professional jai alai players wore an acrylic helmet when on the court. It was the Florida law, the result of a near-death accident during a jai alai game in 1967 in Durango, Spain. Like many of his teammates on the winter season roster at Miami Jai Alai, Fernando Orbea participated in the summer partido season in Spain. Orbea was an accomplished frontcourt player, agile and accurate. But this was jai alai; the ball moved fast from several directions and angles. It was during a match called *pareja contra trio* (two against three) that Orbea was directly in the ball's path. Struck on the temple, his skull fractured, Orbea laid one week in a coma and spent months in rehabilitation. This is why jai alai players wear protective helmets—although there are some who contend helmets interfere with the fear factor, an important component of playing smart. "Before helmets there was only the cesta to defend yourself,

Figure 6.5. "Biscayne Fronton, Home of Jai Alai, Miami, Florida," 1948. Historic Postcard.

and you were always aware you could be hit. And you looked at your opponent's face, watched his expression, his frustration . . . that helped to plan strategy," says professional player Francisco Churruca. "For safety, helmets are best. But jai alai is most intense without helmets."

All in all, the spectacle of athleticism and dazzling shots with the extra action of wagering hooked jai alai fans. In 1975 a record 15,500 fans attended an evening performance at Miami Jai Alai, heralded as "the largest and the most luxurious fronton ever built."

The crowds came to see the top jai alai players, and now Miami claimed one of its own, hometown hero, Joey Cornblit. Joseph "Joey" Cornblit, the son of Israeli immigrants, is almost a Florida native. "I was born in Montreal, Canada, but when I was nine months old, my parents moved to Miami." Cornblit was strong with quick hand-eye coordination, all

Figure 6.6. "The Game," *Miami Jai Alai*, 1970–1971 Season. Jai alai player Joey Cornblit. Courtesy of Joey Cornblit.

attributes of an accomplished athlete. Yet as much as anything else, he had the passion and determination to succeed. "I love the game. I started playing at twelve years old when I was a little skinny kid but was persistent and confident. It's all about confidence," he says.

Cornblit learned to play at North Miami Amateur Jai Alai where promoters of the sport sponsored free instruction for promising young athletes drawn to the speed of jai alai. Coached by Epifanio Saenz, a former player in Cuba, Cornblit played aggressively. "No time for long volleys. Each point is crucial in a fast-rotating round-robin game. If you lose the point, you might not come up a second time on the court. Smash and grab," says Cornblit. He kept his opponents off-balance with a variety of powerful kill shots. "Go for the kill shot. The kill shot is like going into battle with either one bullet or six bullets. A lot better with six shots to win."

Cornblit, an American star in a sport dominated by the Basque, rose to jai alai stardom as the sport caught attention outside of Florida. As much as anyone, Louis Stanley (Buddy) Berenson, whose father fought and won the battle to legalize pari-mutuel jai alai in Florida, raised the sport to new levels of interest beyond the borders of Florida.

"Buddy was all about jai alai," says his son, Richard B. Berenson. As president of Miami Jai Alai—later World Jai Alai— and then owner of Hartford Jai Alai, Buddy Berenson recruited the best players and promoted a variety of betting combinations. Spectators dreaming of big payoffs bet on a player or outcome to win, place, or show. Or, they took a chance with exotic combinations borrowed from horse racing such as exacta, trifecta, quiniela, and the daily double.

Berenson predicted jai alai would be a sellout in states like New York, which ultimately resisted, and Connecticut, which legalized wagering on lotteries, horses, dogs, and jai alai in 1971. "Why not? Jai alai is undergoing its biggest boom in two hundred years and is being played in Jakarta and Hong Kong as well as here (Miami)," he told journalist James Tuite.

Yet jai alai involved gambling, often linked with betting scandals, which led to a backlash against the sport. In 1975 an influence-peddling scandal delayed the launch of jai alai in Connecticut.

Was Tammany Hall in Connecticut, asked those quick to turn against politicians and gamblers? Suspicion of wrongdoing erupted amid rumors of political payoffs to obtain a jai alai gaming license in Bridgeport. The president of Connecticut Sports Enterprises Inc. allegedly paid $250,000 to a

HOW TO WAGER

 Jai-Alai wagering is the same as at a horse track, plus several innovations. You may make any or all of seven different wagers.

WIN: You wager that a team (or singles) will win the game. Tickets are $2 and $5 each.

PLACE: You wager that a team will finish no worse than second. If team wins or comes in 2nd, you receive price shown under "Place" on scoreboard. Tickets are $2 and $5 each.

SHOW: You wager that a team will finish no lower than 3rd. You receive price shown under "Show" on scoreboard. Tickets are $2 and $5 each.

QUINIELA: This is most popular form of wagering. You select two teams to finish in 1—2 order. If they finish that way (regardless of which one wins), you receive quiniela price. Example: if you select teams 2 & 3, you win no matter if finish is 2—3 or 3—2. Tickets are $2 each.

PERFECTA: You wager that two teams will finish in exact order you select. If you wager 2—3, teams must finish in that order. There is no perfecta wagering on the 1st game. Tickets are $3 each.

DAILY DOUBLES: The Daytona Beach Jai Alai fronton has initiated two Daily Doubles on every program. The regular Daily Double on the 3rd and 4th games, remains a $2 double, while the Twilight Double on Matinee days and Midnight Double on Evening programs is a $3 wager and has paid better than $770.00.

"Big Q": See page 4.

Figure 6.7. "How to Wager," *Daytona Beach Jai-Alai (HI-LI) Primer*, 1968.

former Connecticut and national Democratic Party chairman, to move forward the permit from the State Gaming Commission. Ultimately, investigators determined there was no basis for the charges against the local politicians, but the fronton owners did not obtain a state gaming license and sold to new owners. It was not until June 1, 1976, that jai alai opened in Bridgeport, a city with an estimated 17 percent unemployment. Jai alai attracted tourists, added about five hundred jobs, and increased the tax revenue. "Gray Bridgeport looks a lot greener," the mayor said.

In the meantime, less than two weeks earlier on May 19, Miami-based World Jai Alai opened with fanfare a fronton in Hartford, fifty-five miles from Bridgeport. A year later in 1977, only eleven miles from Bridgeport in Milford, Saturday Corporation expanded their jai alai operation in Dania, Florida, to include the architect-designed Milford Jai Alai. The taint of scandal did not go away, however.

The first year at Milford Jai Alai, state prosecutors charged and arrested one player and three bettors with alleged conspiracy to rig the games. They accused the player, who returned to Spain before his arrest, of accepting payments to intentionally lose a game. They accused the coterie of bettors, reportedly members of a gambling group known as the Miami Syndicate, of bribery. The gamblers were known to be systems bettors, a legal betting strategy predicted on statistical analysis. But if a player agreed to throw a game, gamblers privy to the scheme eliminated a player or players out of betting combinations and increased their odds of winning. In the end, the charges were difficult to prove, although fines were levied.

As accusations go, game-fixing in betting sports is a harsh sentence. The scandal began in Connecticut and spread to

Florida where many of the players, owners, operators, and sophisticated gamblers were the same. By 1979, following the arrest of six jai alai people from Florida accused of perjury and game-fixing in Connecticut, Florida governor Robert Graham instigated an investigation of pari-mutuel activities at the ten licensed jai alai frontons in Florida. He appointed Dade County state attorney Janet Reno to coordinate investigations of alleged system betting, game-fixing, and political patronage in the jai alai industry. In February 1980, a Broward County grand jury indicted six former jai alai players and five bettors for alleged game-fixing originating at Dania Jai Alai in Florida. Five of the accused were found guilty.

JAI ALAI IN CONNECTICUT

To this day, I believe there are some people who drove along the interstate highway in Connecticut who thought jai alai was the name of a town. For a quarter century, that was a fitting assumption. Jai alai was a unique and intriguing part of the Connecticut landscape. Then, it became a ghost town and simply disappeared.

I was one of those interstate highway travelers who happened to get off the jai alai exit not long after the sport's arrival in the state. I walked into a fronton—Bridgeport, Exit 28—for the first time in August 1976. On December 12, 2001, I walked out of the Milford fronton having watched the final jai alai game ever played in Connecticut.

What happened in between? You might say it was frenzy, followed by a slow, irreversible fade.

The honeymoon phase lasted from 1976 through 1978, when jai alai and Connecticut were in love with each other.

Packed houses in all three frontons, with Hartford the first to open its doors, followed by Bridgeport and Milford. Enduring memories: the sight of people in Bridgeport lined up at the entrance to sprint into the building, literally knocking each other over to get to prime general admission seats. Cars backed up on the interstate in Milford, the parking booth attendants overwhelmed by the crush of traffic. People crammed shoulder-to-shoulder inside Hartford, standing room crowds the norm every Saturday night.

The attraction was powerful. The game was fast, colorful, and loud. The players were charismatic and possessed a foreign flair. Money flowed through the betting windows. When jai alai first arrived in Connecticut, there was virtually no competition for the gambling dollar. It was a perfect match. A pari-mutuel betting sport in an untapped market. The game was an exciting novelty for first-time fans. Combined attendance in the early years was in the millions.

Then, a new phase. The novelty wears off, but a maturation process begins. Some fans showed up once or twice to satisfy their curiosity and never returned. But there were many others who became dependably loyal and knowledgeable. Fans continued to pump millions through the betting windows, and they began also to connect with the players, whose personalities, style, talents, and quirks became more evident as the years passed.

Then, in April 1988, those players walked out. Picket lines went up in front of the Bridgeport and Hartford frontons as players demanded better working conditions and the recognition of a newly formed union. The frontons remained open by bringing in replacement players. The battle lines were drawn. The damage was done.

Who was right? Who was wrong? Those questions, in

hindsight, are irrelevant. What is indisputable is that whatever forces led the players to turn their backs on management—and vice versa—initiated a death spiral. The picket lines were a powerful barrier. Fans abandoned the sport in droves. Jai alai's days in Connecticut were officially numbered.

If the players' strike was an uppercut, the knockout blow landed several years later. In February 1992, Foxwoods Casino opened in Ledyard, Connecticut. Foxwoods originally planned to close for a few hours each day. But so many people stormed the gaming floors on opening night that the doors remained opened. They have never closed.

Many thousands of the casino-goers were once jai alai regulars. Many more began making the trip to the Mohegan Sun in Uncasville when that casino opened in 1996. Here is the irony: jai alai bills itself, understandably so, as the world's fastest game. Yet, when it comes to the betting aspect, jai alai operates at a snail's pace. The games themselves took, on average, ten to twenty minutes to play. When you are waiting to cash a bet that is an eternity. Compare it to playing a slot machine or a hand of blackjack. Instant gratification wins every time.

The sport was crippled. Management responded by trying to diversify, most notably through efforts to add slot machines to the operation. Those efforts failed. Bridgeport abandoned jai alai entirely in 1995 and converted to a greyhound track. Hartford threw in the towel in 1995. That left one fronton standing: Milford.

A confession: when the patient finally expired, I felt as much relief as sadness. The sight of games being played in front of hundreds of people instead of thousands had become unbearable. As the public relations director at Milford Jai Alai for the better part of twenty years, I was willing at the end to do whatever it took to keep the operation alive. Yet the undertow was overwhelming. Times change. The same market which had embraced jai alai twenty-five years earlier had now forsaken it. There were new, flashier alternatives. It was time to bring down the curtain.

We did that at Milford with a program billed as "Nostalgia Night." More celebration than funeral, thousands of fans turned out for one of the final Saturday performances of the fronton's existence. There were souvenir giveaways. There was a ceremony retiring the number of Milford's first great star, Juaristi. Mostly, though, there was reflection.

Fans, players, and employees knew the sand in the hourglass had run out. Yet a different type of energy ran through the building that night, an urge to somehow keep things going. But there would be no reprieve. Jai alai in Connecticut had been reduced to a longing for what once was. It was not coming back.

Consider, though, what was lost. Connecticut had something you could find almost nowhere else. Jai alai breathed a different kind of life into the region. There was the excitement that came with learning about a new sport, a fabulous game without peer. The fascination of discovering a different people and culture, the Basques of Spain and France. The energy, noise, and color of a pari-mutuel facility on a crowded night, fans riding with their bets on every point.

Those lucky enough to experience it will never forget it. The final exit arrived too quickly.

> —Bob Heussler, Radio and Television Sportscaster
> Based in New York City and the Former Director of
> Public Relations at Milford Jai Alai

Still, even with questions about the sport's integrity, the crowds came to watch and bet on jai alai. It was true, jai alai as a fast-action betting sport appealed to fans. "Those early years, it was absolutely electrifying. Saturday nights in Milford, people lined up at the door dozens deep. By the final game of the night the place would be going crazy," says Bob Heussler, former public relations director at Milford Jai Alai.

But people across the United States missed the opportunity to see the game because jai alai never got off the ground as a nationally televised sports event. Instead, jai alai made national television as a juicy tabloid-style story. It seemed with success came scandals. On June 21, 1979, television reporter Geraldo Rivera presented a seventeen-minute segment about jai alai on *20/20*, an ABC prime-time news magazine. "Jai Alai: License to Steal" was about corruption. The piece fit the news formula, a controversy of public concern to patrons, taxpayers, regulators, and of course, politicians who voted for the gambling tax revenue. But because this was about their integrity and honesty, the proud Basque jai alai players felt Rivera's special report about some "rotten apples" in the betting sport made more of the acknowledged wrongdoing than was deserved. "For us it [jai alai] is not just a job or a sport, it is life. Our fathers and grandfathers were in jai alai. What has happened in the last few years we just can't take," said professional player Fernando Orbea to the St. Petersburg *Evening Independent*.

An investigative reporter raises questions. Rivera reported the joint inquiries initiated in 1977 by Connecticut and picked up by Florida in 1979 on wagering irregularities. He asked whether high-roller system bettors conspire with players to fix games. Was management involved? Then Rivera shifted his attention to December 26, 1978, the morning Palm Beach Jai Alai burned, an unsolved act of arson. Was the fire linked to insurance fraud, and why were the gambling records buried? Though there was no proof of improprieties in the records, the implication was clear. Players, owners, handicappers, clerks, concessionaires, security officers, regulators—all the elements associated with the big-money betting sport of jai alai faced suspicion.

False, true, or half-true, the aura of corruption stuck. "Winning over the skeptics was futile. Many people had their minds made up before they watched even a game or two. I accepted that. People saw a game you could bet on which was played by humans. Nothing more ripe for skepticism than that. But many years after the fact I will look you in the eye and tell you this: the game was honest," says Heussler.

But there were other troubles that impacted the sport.

7
TROUBLED JAI ALAI

On May 27, 1981, John "The Executioner" Martorano killed World Jai Alai owner Roger Wheeler in the parking lot of Southern Hills Country Club in Tulsa, Oklahoma. Shortly after four o'clock in the afternoon after his usual Wednesday round of golf, Wheeler walked to his car and opened the door of the black Cadillac. Martorano, wearing a fake black beard, tinted glasses, and baseball hat, got out of his beige Pontiac, walked to the Cadillac, and shot Wheeler between the eyes at such close range that the impact of the bullet embedded bits of Wheeler's glasses in Wheeler's eyes. The getaway driver drove up to the scene, Martorano jumped in the car, and they fled. The hunt began. Who wanted Wheeler dead? And why?

Roger Wheeler was a savvy millionaire entrepreneur who built his fortune from oil and electronics. At the time of his murder he was chairman of Telex Corporation, manufacturer of communications terminals and computer equipment, and owner of World Jai Alai Inc., the largest network of professional jai alai frontons in the United States. Always on the alert for profitable investment opportunities, Wheeler had looked into a racetrack, the slot-machine business, and a Las Vegas casino. But it was the gambling sport of jai alai that caught his eye and money; Miami-based World Jai Alai, with frontons in Florida and Connecticut, showed net profits of five million dollars a year on revenues of over thirty million dollars, and the First National Bank of Boston promised a fifty-million-dollar loan package. In 1978 Wheeler entered the booming jai alai business. Wheeler personally was not fond of gambling, and the huge payoffs of pari-mutuel wagering were often the target of suspicions of corruption. But "he thought his business acumen could override the 'shady characters,'" note journalists Dick Lehr and Gerald O'Neill.

Instead, "shady characters" hastened Wheeler's demise. Several relevant to World Jai Alai bear mentioning, including the gunman, Martorano. A known hitman, he turned government witness in 2013 as part of a plea deal and confessed to twenty murders, among them Roger Wheeler's. "I didn't enjoy killing anybody. I enjoyed helping a friend if I could," he said. Martorano referred to his "friend," organized crime leader James "Whitey" Bulger. Bulger and his partner Stephen Flemmi controlled the Winter Hill Gang headquartered in Boston, Massachusetts, where they protected their far-flung criminal interests with murder, if necessary. Those criminal interests included gambling and jai alai.

An alleged fraternizer with members of the Winter Hill Gang, John Callahan was not only a CPA but also a business consultant to Boston investors. As president of World Jai Alai before Wheeler's acquisition of the company, behind the scenes Callahan maintained his established contacts and interest in the company. The FBI implicated Callahan in making and laundering money for Bulger, but before Callahan could be questioned about his involvement, in 1982 he was shot in the back of the head, his body found in the trunk of his Cadillac at the Miami International Airport.

When he took over the company, Wheeler retained World Jai Alai's vice president for security Paul Rico, a retired FBI agent specializing in organized crime. Eventually, in 2003 Florida investigators in Oklahoma and Florida indicted Rico on charges for helping Bulger and Flemmi plan Wheeler's assassination. In 2004 Rico died in custody before his trial.

A key moment in Wheeler's fate occurred during a Winter Hill meeting in Boston in early January 1981. There was a problem. "The hard-driving CEO from Oklahoma had 'discovered something was not right,'" report Lehr and O'Neill. Wheeler suspected someone was skimming cash from the jai alai proceeds, possibly from food and parking concessions and unreported bets. He planned to replace part of the management team, including two financial officers, with people he trusted. Wheeler was in Bulger's way.

"Take [Wheeler] out of the box." Edward "Brian" Halloran, loan shark collector for the Winter Hill Gang, informed the FBI that this was a reference to shooting Wheeler in the head. In 1982 Halloran exited a Boston bar, walked to his car, and was shot and killed.

Ultimately, Martorano admitted he shot Wheeler on orders from his bosses at Winter Hill. It was his testimony that helped convict Bulger of racketeering charges and a role in the murders of eleven people. In 2013 after sixteen years on the run, Bulger was sentenced to two consecutive life sentences plus five years. The "scope, callousness and depravity of your crimes are almost unfathomable . . . made all the more heinous because they were all about money," said Judge Denise Casper of the federal district court to Bulger, who was standing to receive his sentence. In 2015 Hollywood recreated the bloody 1981 murder of Wheeler in the movie about Bulger, *Black Mass*.

GAMBLING, JAI ALAI, AND MURDER

Under my father's guidance, I ran the initial financial analysis on World Jai Alai before the purchase. Today you would use a spreadsheet, but back then I had to write a custom computer program. If memory serves me correctly, WJA looked so profitable that it could repay its purchase price in around five years. After the business went in decline, Dad told me he was going to change management. By having him shot, ex-FBI agent H. Paul Rico was able to stay in place. WJA continued its decline and was never able to repay the bank debt used for the purchase. About twenty years later, the banks forced us to sell.

I have always believed ex-FBI agent H. Paul Rico was behind my father's murder. He had the means, motive, and opportunity. The most troubling part of my father's murder was how, for nearly two decades, the FBI and the Department of Justice did everything possible to protect him from police investigation. Without the bulldogged determination of Sgt. Michael Huff and the help of countless police officers from Connecticut, Florida, Massachusetts, and Oklahoma, this murder would never have been solved. The police investigation ended with the arrest of this ex-FBI agent for my father's murder. Rico died under suspicious circumstances awaiting trial.

—David Wheeler, son of Roger Wheeler

●

Skimming and laundering money was a crime racket that had nothing to do with the classic game of jai alai, but jai alai as a professional sport took a hit from the adverse publicity generated by Wheeler's gangland assassination. Even so, fronton owners continued to earn profits, states reaped revenues, players dreamed of American stardom, and fans watched the games and bet.

So what happened to jai alai at the time when the sport seemed to be positioned to catch on in the United States? "Jai alai was growing. We saw endless growth. The undoing began in 1988 when the players went on strike. It was devastating," says Richard Berenson, whose father, Stanley Berenson, owned Hartford Jai Alai in Connecticut. Berenson grew up with jai alai in a fronton family spanning three generations. "I played amateur jai alai until the ball hit me, shattered my left ankle. No more," he says.

In 1988 the jai alai association of professional players in the United States called a strike in a dispute over benefits. "The strike was nasty. Picket lines drove away fans," says Berenson. On day eleven of the strike, the Connecticut Division of Special Revenue temporarily closed the Hartford and Bridgeport frontons because angry and frustrated strikers harassed fans and the replacement players. The replacements—established players who crossed the picket line, amateurs with little or no professional experience—kept the games going, but the intensity of the play suffered and attendance plummeted. Strikers lost income, frontons lost cash flow, and states lost wagering revenue. "By the end of the strike, many of the fans who left did not return. There were no winners. Everyone lost, players and management," says Richard Berenson.

Player strikes in other sports had happened before and will happen again. In 1972, Major League Baseball (MLB) canceled 86 games; in 1987, 713 games; and from 1994–1995 the entire MLB season was canceled. In 2011 the National Basketball Association (NBA) delayed the start of the season, reducing the number of games during the regular season. The sports felt the impact, financial and otherwise, but there was no permanent, devastating loss in their popularity with fans. Jai alai, on the fringe of the mainstream, could not fall back on a national sport image or a passionate fan base buttressed by grassroots youth programs and regional team rivalry.

"The real beauty of jai alai is watching them play. It's an art," says Marty Fleischman, former public relations director for World Jai Alai. While it is true that tradition-rich jai alai is enjoyed for its own sake, American professional jai alai marketed itself as an exciting spectator sport designed for pari-mutuel wagering. By the time the strike ended in 1991, Native Americans operated casinos on tribal land, cruise ships offered offshore gambling, and states held lotteries more profitable for them than sports betting. Jai alai competed amid new and less expensive to maintain entertainment and gambling options. Attendance and money wagered declined, and frontons closed.

In 1995, Hartford and Bridgeport Jai Alai folded. "No pari-mutuel jai alai can compete with a casino's fast action," said Hartford owner Stanley Berenson. In 2001 Milford Jai Alai closed. And so twenty-six years of jai alai in Connecticut ended. Only Newport Jai Alai in Rhode Island remained open for fans in the Northeast, but by 2003 jai alai at Newport was gone, replaced with more than a thousand video slot machines and simulcast races on the casino floor at Newport Grand.

Jai alai players lost their jobs. Some of the Basque players returned to their native Spain or France. Most players hoped to remain in the United States where the pay was good and the season long. But the demand was low. By the beginning of the '90s, the network of frontons that supported hundreds of professional players had diminished to a smaller version of its former self.

Nevada frontons had already closed. Even though gambling revenues in 1975 earned more than one billion dollars annually, casino patrons preferred the familiar forms of casino gambling and entertainment to jai alai. Why wait twelve or fifteen minutes for the outcome of a jai alai match when round-the-clock table poker or slot machines produce almost instant results? Casino-goers said, jai alai is a slow way to lose or win money . . . and what is a *chula* shot? In 1980 the Las Vegas MGM Grand Hotel with adjoining fronton burned in a disastrous fire. Owner Kirk Kerkorian reopened his hotel, but this time without jai alai. That same year jai alai failed to reach Kerkorian's expectations at the MGM Grand in Reno, and the games ended after a two-year run.

So pro players like Leon "Tevin" Shepard from Milford Jai Alai jostled for frontcourt positions in a crowded player's marketplace. Shepard, who once played center field on his high school baseball team in Bridgeport, Connecticut, says, "From the first time I borrowed a cesta and threw the ball hard and it landed straight down on the floor, bounced back and hit me in the face, requiring stitches, I knew I wanted to play jai alai." Jai alai was a challenge. He worked hard to become skilled at the sport he did not grow up playing. It paid off. When the last of Connecticut's three frontons closed, Shepard earned a spot on the roster at Miami Jai Alai.

Out-of-work players turned to Florida, the state that once

Figure 7.1. Tijuana Jai Alai, Tijuana, Mexico, 1960s. Historic Postcard.

welcomed jai alai with as many as a dozen professional frontons. But jai alai continued to bleed. In 1990 Big Bend Jai Alai in Quincy and Melbourne Jai Alai closed, followed by Daytona Beach in 1992. West Palm Beach closed in 1994, and Tampa Jai Alai in 1998. Across the US border and in Mexico, jai alai was no longer a career option. By the end of the decade, the large palatial-like frontons in Mexico City and Tijuana were empty landmarks.

As a professional sport, jai alai in the United States was no longer economically viable. By 2008 only two frontons in Florida, Miami and Dania, played year-round jai alai. The remaining four—Fort Pierce, Ocala, Orlando, and Jasper—offered seasonal games, sufficient to satisfy the Florida law that coupled the specific pari-mutuel gambling license with horse and dog racing and jai alai venues.

What happens when a jai alai player cannot play? When he is in the middle of his career and out of work? When he is not in demand? This is who he is, a professional athlete who dedicates his life to rigorous training and competition. Jai alai player Robert Barrios says, "I love what I do." He wants to keep playing.

In 1980 Barrios was one year old, and his family moved from Havana, Cuba, to Miami, Florida. "Things were getting worst in Cuba and my father wanted something better for his family." His father was not alone in his choice: between April 15 and October 31 in 1980 more than a hundred thousand Cuban refugees arrived in Florida during the Mariel Boatlift.

Barrios was ten years old when he first played jai alai. "After my mother died when I was nine, my older sister thought taking jai alai lessons would be fun for me. It was her idea." By that time, jai alai in Miami was popular and growing, entrenched, it seemed, in Florida as a mainstream sport. His sister, whose husband introduced her to jai alai, passed his love of the sport to her. Barrios's father, who heard stories about the breathtaking athleticism and wild betting that had occurred at the defunct Havana Jai Alai, never saw a game in Cuba, but in Miami he got his chance. Most everyone visiting or living in Miami knew about the games at Miami Jai Alai.

Like most children growing up in his neighborhood in South Beach, Barrios joined his friends after school to play baseball, and sometimes basketball or football. He was a good all-around athlete. "But jai alai caught my eye. Jai alai was different . . . the twist of the cesta, the ball flying at me, the speed of the game. I fell in love with it," he says.

Barrios, along with fifty to sixty other age-group students, trained at the North Miami Amateur Court created to attract young local players. Otherwise, Americans categorized jai alai as a Basque sport played by Basque players trained in

Basque facilities in Spain. Coached by José Barena, a former player from Cuba, Barrios learned to put a spin on the ball and place his shots. He learned to watch his opponent, thinking, "What am I going to throw back?" Initially, he practiced with a plastic cesta, then a used wicker cesta, and eventually his own cesta, imported from Spain and paid from his savings. Each practice, Barrios's father was there, courtside. After working the night shift as an accountant at the Fontainbleau Hotel in Miami Beach, his father slept a few hours, picked up his son from school, drove him to practice, stayed to watch him play, and snatched a cat nap at home before going to work in the evening. A couple times a week father and son drove to amateur practice sessions at the West Palm Beach fronton so that Barrios sharpened his game sense on a long regulation-size court.

When Barrios was fifteen years old, his father died. When Barrios was eighteen years old, he received his first professional jai alai contract. He selected his game name, "Tico" (Little Robertico), his childhood nickname. He proved he could play in Dania, Florida, transferred to Newport Jai Alai in Rhode Island, and came full circle to play in his hometown at Miami Jai Alai. "My father always wanted me to learn the game well enough to play professionally. I am proud I made it for me and my father. I think of my father when I play," says Barrios.

Typically a pro jai alai player begins to feel the effect of injuries and aging by the time he reaches his forties. What does an athlete do for an encore after retirement from active play? "Jai alai is my life's work. My dream is to teach jai alai to the next generation of young players," says Barrios. Here is the rub. The decline of American jai alai stressed by financial and cultural pressures casts doubt on the future of jai alai, on or off the court. Today these elite athletes often find themselves forced to prepare for another career path, reconstructing their lifestyle and identity.

IS JAI ALAI DYING?

To try to understand the current situation of the jai alai world in the United States and Basque Country it helps to go back in memory to the old days when the sport was so successful.

In the early 1970s Friday and Saturday nights at Miami Jai Alai and Tampa Jai Alai were standing-room only. Full capacity at Miami, the mecca of jai alai, was more than ten thousand spectators; in Tampa, more than nine thousand.

Initially, jai alai in Florida was a seasonal sport, each fronton licensed in a specific locale for the winter or summer season. Fans looked forward to the return of the game after an absence of almost half a year.

After 1973 successful jai alai companies expanded. World Jai Alai, the parent company of Miami Jai Alai, purchased the fronton at Tampa, opened a new one at Ocala, and then opened one at Fort Pierce. The corporate leaders completed the rosters at their increased holdings with combinations of players formed from Miami and Tampa. Thus, for the first time in Florida the players of a company were employed full-time, year-round. By the end of the decade jai alai spread from Florida to Nevada, Connecticut, and Rhode Island.

This demand for professional players throughout the year in the United States created a big vacuum in Basque Spain, the "crib" of the jai alai world, because it was customary for the Basque players to return to their homeland to play the summer season when the American winter/spring season ended. But now in frontons like Guernica, Markina, and Durango, the fans did not have the luxury of watching their sons and friends play for them during the summer. This greatly contributed to the decline of the jai alai fan base in the Basque region of Spain.

So what happened in the United States where jai alai was so popular? In my opinion, once Florida permitted all the frontons to remain open year-round, this stole the hunger for jai alai from the fan base that kept them enthusiastic during the short, limited seasons.

In 1988 the players in the United States formed a players' association, IJAPA (International Jai Alai Players Association) and went on strike. (I retired the year just before the strike.) The strike lasted three years, but the frontons remained open. The jai alai companies were able to recruit new players, most of whom would never have been able to play professionally under normal circumstances (talent did not matter). Attendance became smaller and smaller. There were no winners on either side. Around that time, Florida introduced the state lottery. This gave the average citizen the option to bet outside the legal channels of jai alai, horse tracks, and dog tracks.

Jai alai as a sport was in decline. The owners of the frontons looked for ways to increase their revenue. In time, the state of Florida granted permits to operate table card games and inter-track wagering at the frontons. Today, jai alai is the small, poor brother of big gambling interests. They need jai alai because this is how they "grandfather" in with their pari-mutuel sport license to operate casino-style gambling. It is a sad solution and an insult to this honorable and unique sport.

So what is the solution? Unfortunately, I don't see one, unless the jai alai industry stands alone as an independent entity. Only allow betting on the game, the way it used to be. Advertise to create a new wave of fans. Break the playing year into seasons to avoid overexposure. Interest today's youngsters to learn the sport. It is a long process with no demand and pay incentive from the struggling jai alai companies.

—José M. Goitia,
Professional Jai Alai Player from 1963–1987

In August 2013, Miami Jai Alai Casino filed for bankruptcy. "The assets of Florida Gaming Corp., including the casino at Miami Jai Alai, will be auctioned off through bankruptcy on March 25," announced the *South Florida Business Journal*. In the end the casino's lead creditor ABC Funding paid $155 million to buy the historic fronton enhanced with a sixty-thousand-square-foot casino. As the casino part of the business propelled the profits, a diminished jai alai moved to second billing. Miami Jai Alai Casino became Casino Miami Jai Alai, and eventually, Casino Miami, owned and operated by Fronton Holdings LLC, a nod to the staying power—for the time being—of jai alai in Florida. For the Florida gaming law linked pari-mutuel jai alai with a license to offer casino-style slot machines and card-table poker in the same building as the fronton—which is how jai alai in Dania, Florida, got back in the business.

"Sometimes the sign of progress is a completely gutted building," says *Sun Sentinel* reporter Nick Sortal. In 2015, a group of Argentine investors partnered with the Magic City Casino group from Miami to make over the Dania Casino & Jai Alai into a special destination. On January 13, 2016, the new owners unveiled The Casino at Dania Beach, a twenty-first century Dania Jai Alai. The new face of the old Dania Jai Alai retained a modicum of jai alai, but the highest priority was to attract a new generation of consumers with slot machines, poker tables, electronic gaming, simulcast betting, a sports bar, and restaurants and concerts. "I want people to come to The Casino at Dania Beach for more than the slots, for other amenities . . . to dine at a good restaurant, see a show, and watch an entertaining game of jai alai," says Dania CEO Scott Savin.

Sixty, fifty, forty years ago jai alai fans packed the five-thousand-seat Dania fronton, evenings and matinees, to watch and wager on a thrilling show of star athletes. On this opening day of Dania's transformation, loyal fans who remembered and missed good times at Dania Jai Alai scattered through the modified 550-seat fronton. Or, casino patrons played the slot machines, watched the jai alai action on a large video screen on the slot floor, and intrigued, placed a wager. "I want to repackage jai alai and make a unique game with great athletes better. From a business standpoint I will give jai alai my best shot to make it work," says Savin.

HOW I SEE IT

I've always had a vision of making jai alai great again. When I was a young boy growing up in Miami, every weekend my parents attended the games at Miami Jai Alai. Eventually my uncle, who was a very good amateur player in the 1970s, convinced my father to learn to play jai alai. After a couple of years of going with my father and uncle to the amateur facility, I decided to give it a try. Ever since I never stopped playing the game. When I was fifteen years old, and I was playing high school baseball and basketball, my jai alai instructor asked my parents if they would consider letting me play jai alai exclusively. Two years later I became a professional player.

I have played professionally at all the frontons in the United States, and during the 1990s participated in tournaments in Spain and France. There have always been companies and federations that put on excellent jai alai tournaments in the summer months in Europe. There is a lot of competition as well from these companies and federations. This is no different than any other industry. The sport of jai alai has been struggling for years to maintain a presence in their respected areas. Companies try to outdo the previous companies. Competition is good for all industries. However, in the jai alai industry it has created some damage by separating the small group of people that should actually be working together to make the sport great.

I began working as players' manager at Dania Jai Alai in 2009, and I take the approach of thinking globally but acting locally. We at Dania have had some of the best players in the world. From time to time when asked to participate in these global events, we gladly send our players so they can represent Dania jai alai.

I think that Dania is in a position of opportunity to make the sport popular in the Broward County area. I also believe that the game itself has a great opportunity because of the players that are currently playing and the players that will be coming to play here soon. We have a very young and exciting roster that if given the opportunity can perform for many years to come. We also have an opportunity at Dania because the new casino, concert venue, and restaurants will bring more foot traffic to the fronton than ever before. People that are coming to visit for other entertainment purposes can walk into the jai alai area and fulfill their curiosity.

Dania has always had a very strong fan base of die-hard aficionados. These two hundred to three hundred diehards create a good foundation for keeping things going for years to come. In the 1970s and '80s, the sport was at the height of its popularity. We lost a little bit of our fan base due to the fact that we didn't keep up with the changing trends. Nowadays, it is much tougher to attract the entertainment dollar. You have to be special and give excellent customer service so your customers will enjoy their experience and return to your facility. Now Dania Jai Alai has a marketing and promotion team in place that is going to market the property as a unit. They are going to market their casino, their restaurants and their entertainment, including jai alai, as a whole. That should create a larger fan base for the sport.

In 2016, after the renovations, we had nine professionals who decided to retire. This gave us a great opportunity of filling those roster spots with young debutantes that would be coming to America for the first time to start their professional career. We had two choices in making the decision to fill the spots. The first choice was to go with seasoned veterans that play around the world and have proven to be some of the best players available that are not currently on a United States roster. The second option was to go to the jai alai schools in the Basque Country and select the best amateur players available. My decision was to select nine amateur players in an attempt to build a strong group of young players that can play at Dania for the next decade or two. Our selection includes four World Amateur Gold medalists and four of the top amateur players in the world. It also includes one seasoned veteran to complete our feature game lineup. Through coaching and training, the plan is to build these players to become superstars on our roster.

What makes jai alai important to me and the reason that I am sticking with it today is because when I was young, there were several people that helped develop me into who I have become today. As I got a bit older and I looked back on the times in the beginning of my career, I became more and more grateful for these people and what they have done for me. In a sense, my motivation today is to pay it forward. I was fortunate to play in an era of greatness for the sport of jai alai. I feel that I am in the position to help make this sport great again. I think that this sport has all the potential to be as good or better than sports like baseball, basketball, tennis, or any other mainstream sport. The main ingredient that those sports have that jai alai needs to work on is exposure.

I feel that if given the opportunity, I can help . . .

—Ben Bueno, Professional Jai Alai player

Epilogue

I stood on the serving line of the short practice court at Connecticut Amateur Jai Alai in Berlin, Connecticut. I strapped a worn wicker cesta onto my right wrist, bounced a hard plastic ball wrapped with electrical tape, scooped it up in my cesta, and threw toward the concrete block front wall, painted green epoxy. My wrist flopped and the ball dropped. Yet I sensed the momentum of a perfect swing, the speed of the ball, the spin off the wall, the excitement of the crowd. I thought about the rich history of jai alai rooted in the ancient Basque Country in the Western Pyrenees Mountains of Spain and France. Jai alai brought to mind the tradition of Old World Basque Ball with its art of boldness and skill, and its culture of community and competition, and also, betting. But because jai alai is played out on the American sport scene I wonder about the future of jai alai defined by commercialization and legalized gambling.

Jai alai remains part of fringe American sports scene, though now many of the players are devoted amateurs rather than professional players, all playing for the love of the game.

"I was blown away when I saw my first professional jai alai. It was in 2011, and I made the trip from my home in Connecticut to the Citrus Tournament in Orlando, Florida. The play was so much faster than I expected. It was also the first time I bet on jai alai, which was thrilling. I was instantly hooked and wished that professional jai alai was still in Connecticut," says amateur player Katie DiDomizio, who acquired her love of the game from her father, former professional player Matt DiDomizio.

"When I was a young girl, pretty much every time my Dad and I went grocery shopping my Dad parked the car behind the store and batted a bunch of balls against the lot wall with his cesta . . . for thirty minutes, maybe an hour, or until the manager yelled at him and told him to leave. My Dad would chase the balls into the woods and climb onto roofs to get down the balls. I'd be in the car begging him to hurry up. Even if we were driving somewhere, and my Dad saw a wall that would be good for playing jai alai, he would stop to check it out. I used to think he had lost his mind."

Matt DiDomizio simply was frustrated. He wanted to play a real game of jai alai on a real court. On May 1, 2010, DiDomizio, a postal employee, opened Connecticut Amateur Jai Alai, an amateur fronton in a converted warehouse in Berlin, Connecticut. "There is something about the game of jai alai that can't be described. It instills a passion in you which does not go away. Maybe it's the excitement, the skill, the danger, the grace. I was frustrated when I, and others, could no longer enjoy this beautiful sport in Connecticut. So I risked everything, mortgaged my house, and did what no one thought possible and destined to fail—I built a jai alai court. Why? I just wanted to play jai alai," says DiDomizio. Ten years after Milford Jai Alai, the remaining fronton in

Connecticut, closed, the sport of jai alai played by professional players made its comeback as amateur play.

That is how Katie DiDomizio learned to play jai alai. "The first day on court I tried throwing around the ball, and my brother and Steve Rastocky, an ex-pro, showed me how to throw a forehand and backhand. After that, I watched the players and perfected my throws. As I began to play more, some guys would tell me how to improve my game. Churruca taught me how to throw a 'rebote,' which is when you return the ball when it comes off the back wall. That was amazing. For all of you sports fans, that would be as if Michael Jordan taught you how to throw free throws. Simply amazing. I was being taught by royalty."

Today with the decline of jai alai, the idea of amateur jai alai as a stepping-stone to professional play in the United States seems somewhat improbable. Yet at the peak of jai alai's popularity in the 1970s and '80s, amateurs became pros. "Of about 500 professional jai alai players in this country, more than 100 started here (North Miami Amateur Jai Alai)," reported the Broward County *Sun-Sentinel* in 1988. All of them were men, though North Miami Amateur Becky Smith wanted to become jai alai's first female professional player.

"I grew up with jai alai. Jai alai to me is like football to another person. My mother worked at jai alai, my father loves to go to jai alai, and I grew up hearing about all these great players like Joey and Pierre. Another reason I guess I play the sport is that it's a Basque sport and my great-grandfather was Basque," Smith told journalist Darlene Gardner. In 1987 Smith qualified to compete at the Amateur Gold Coast Jai Alai Championships at Dania, Florida. What next?

Smith missed the opportunity to pursue her campaign. What if the three-year players' strike that began in 1988 had not interrupted the momentum of a burgeoning sports industry . . . what if game-fixing scandals had not turned away disgusted betting fans . . . what if casino competition had not siphoned off jai alai's foundational strength? But it did. Today, Florida is the only state where professional jai alai action survives, and even then, playing time is limited and the frontons few.

So where does jai alai go from here? Enhanced by globalization, which originally enabled a centuries-old rural Basque tradition to spread throughout the world as a distinctive international sport, jai alai has increasingly struggled to be relevant in today's largely homogeneous corporate sports worldview that seems to have little place for novelty. The future is uncertain, to say the least.

Did globalization strengthen the tradition of jai alai or simplify it? It would appear to be the latter. With the focus on fast games and pari-mutuel betting, pieces of this beautiful and complex sport were simplified for a broader audience. Jai alai is our sport, say the Basque. Yet today in the Basque Country jai alai falters, too. In the summer, the top jai alai players pair off in action-packed tournament matches that attract vacationers in the French seaside town of Saint-Jean-De-Luz. But from the mountain town of Markina, Spain, to the riverfront city of Bilbao, Spain, once fashionable world-class jai alai frontons packed with thousands of spectators struggle to maintain facilities and retain fans while *pelota a mano*, played with bare hand (an inexpensive piece of equipment), is a popular professional sport covered on Basque television. Even so, like Euskara, the language of the Basque, and txapela, the Basque beret, jai alai—in all its complexity—is an integral part of Basque culture, and this keeps it alive.

Glossary

cancha: Playing court.

cesta: Long, curved, woven-reed basket used to catch and throw the ball in jai alai games.

cesta punta: Basque term for game of jai alai.

chic-chac shot: The ball hits the floor next to or in the angle of the back wall and floor, creating little or no bounce.

chistera: Short, light, reed basket scoop, an early version of the cesta.

chula shot: The ball hits the lower part of the back wall and comes out with an extremely low bounce, difficult to catch.

dos paredes, the carom shot: The player throws the ball so it hits the sidewall, the front wall, and then hits inbounds toward the outside of the court.

Euskara: The Basque language, also spelled Euskera.

frontis: Front wall of the playing court.

fronton: Building, or arena, where jai alai is played.

jai alai: A variant of the Basque handball court game played with a cesta (reed basket) used to throw and catch a hard rubber ball (pelota) against the wall; in Basque, the word means "Merry Festival."

pari-mutuel wagering: "The method of setting payoffs employed in horse racing and jai alai that dispenses with a central odds maker in favor of dividing the betting pool among the holders of winning tickets" (Skiena, *Calculated Bets*).

partido: A point-by-point jai alai game played to a preset thirty or thirty-five points, occasionally forty points, by two teams, each with two players; jai alai is typically played in Spain in long partidos.

pelota: Goatskin-covered hard rubber ball.

pelota a mano: A Basque handball game played with a hard rubber ball hit with the bare hand.

pelota a pala: A Basque handball game played with a flat wood paddle (pala) used to hit a hard rubber ball.

pelota a peleta (paleta Argentina): Argentine Basque paddle ball (pelota a pala).

pelotari: Jai alai player.

pelota vasca: Generic term for all varieties of Basque Ball.

quiniela: "Because of the wagering system, jai alai is played in the United States in a different fashion from the long partido sessions in Spain: The game in the United States is called quiniela and can be played in singles, doubles, or, at times, three players on each team: Most quinielas are composed of eight teams, although this is not the rule; six or seven teams may also complete" (Goitia, *The Other Side of the Screen*).

rebote shot: The player returns the ball coming off the back wall.

remate shot: This is any kill shot, a "put-away" shot.

Spectacular Seven scoring method: Games played to seven points in professional jai alai in the United States speed the pace of the game by doubling the point value after each team takes one turn through the initial rotation; each point counts for one point in the first round and counts for two points in the second round.

Notes

The notes cited here are a guide for the reader who wants to explore the cultural history of jai alai. Full bibliographic information for these sources is in the selected bibliography.

Preface

"The globalization of sports is part of a much larger—and much more controversial—globalization process," is derived from "Globalization and Sports Processes," discussed in "Sports," *Encyclopedia Britannica Online*, https://www.britannica.com/topic/Sports.

Chapter 1

For the plot, cast, and crew of the *Miami Vice* episode of "Kill Shot" televised on October 10, 1986, see http://www.imdb.com/title/tt0647084/fullcredits/. Through interviews and correspondence, Marty Fleishman, former public relations director for World Jai Alai Inc., relates his story of the production of "Kill Shot" on location at Miami Jai Alai.

A sense of South Florida at the time of *Miami Vice* is drawn from Allman, *Miami: City of the Future*; James Kelly, "South

Florida: Trouble in Paradise," *TIME Magazine*, November 23, 1981; Paul S. George, "Miami: One Hundred Years of History," *Miami Archives*, http://www.historymiami.org/research-miami/topics/history-of-miami/.

For Ernest Hemingway's comment about jai alai, "It is a grand sport," see Geoffrey Gray, "In Basque Country, Coming Home to Jai Alai," *New York Times*, May 14, 2006. "So Jai Alai must be a great game" is taken from "Jai-Alai Is Popular but Hard to Explain," *St. Petersburg Times*, March 10, 1946.

"For me, jai alai is everything," says jai alai player Iñaki Goikoetxea through personal interviews and correspondence.

"When I threw the first ball I instantly fell in love with the sport," says jai alai player Juan Arrasate through interviews and correspondence.

Chapter 2

The overview of the history and culture of the Basque follows Douglass and Zulaika, *Basque Culture: Anthropological Perspectives*; Gallop, *A Book of Basques*; Kurlansky, *The Basque History of the World*; Woodworth, *The Basque Country: A Cultural History*.

"I would like to invite you to pronounce the longest surname in Euzkara, Iturriberrigorrigoikoerrotakoetxea" is found in Goitia, *Jai Alai, The Other Side of the Screen*.

"Basque pelota was one of these cultural icons which served both as a form of recreation and as a cultural sacrament" is derived from Urza, *Historia de la Pelota Vasca en las Americas (The History of Basque Pelota in the Americas)*. For the history of jai alai rooted in the tradition of Basque Ball, see Abrisketa, *Basque Pelota: A Ritual, an Aesthetic*; Blazy, *La Pelote Basque*; Perallón, *Pelota Vasca*; Goitia, *Jai Alai, The Other Side of the Screen*.

"I do not remember how old I was when I started to play jai alai but I do know that cestas were among my first toys," says jai alai player José Goitia through interviews and correspondence.

To view "Land of the Basques," the documentary made by filmmaker Orson Welles for the BBC (British Broadcast Company) in 1955, see https://www.youtube.com/watch?v=hJIKx3NPuts.

Chapter 3

"I do not understand how these heavy balls are so elastic that when they touch the ground even though lightly thrown, they spring into the air with the most incredible leaps," is derived from the early Spanish accounts collected by Martyr d'Anghera, *De Orbe Novo* (*On the New World*). The history of the Mesoamerica native rubber plant and natural rubber processing used to make rubber game balls is drawn from Hosler, and Burkett, and Tarkanian, *Prehistoric Polymers: Rubber Processing in Ancient Mesoamerica*; Scarborough and Wilcox, eds., *The Mesoamerican Ballgame*; Stern, *The Rubber Ball Games of the Americas*; Whittington, ed., *The Sport of Life and Death: The Mesoamerican Ballgame*.

For the role of the Argentina Basque in the evolution of the modern cesta, see Abrisketa, *Basque Pelota: A Ritual, an Aesthetic*; Blazy, *La Pelote Basque*; Douglass and Bilbao, *Amerikanuak: Basques in the New World*; Koebel, *Modern Argentina: The El Dorado of To-Day*; Perallón, *Pelota Vasca*; Totoricagüena, *Basque Diaspora: Migration and Transnational Identity*; Urza, *Historia de la Polta en las Americas*.

"Buying a cesta is like buying your wife gold jewelry . . . valuable, expensive and personal," says jai alai player Francisco Churruca through interviews and correspondence.

Present-day cesta maker Carlos Campo, and jai alai ballmakers Miguel Altuna and Clementé Garcia, describe and demonstrate their craft through interviews at Miami Jai Alai.

Chapter 4

"What the theater is to New York jai alai is to Havana" is derived from Dorothy Stanhope, "Jai Alai: Havana's Favorite Recreation," *New York Times*, January 17, 1904. The overview of the history and culture of jai alai in Cuba follows Bethell, *Cuba: A Short History*; Dana, *To Cuba and Back*; Méndez Muñiz, *La Pelota Vasca En Cuba: Su Evolucion Hasta 1930* (Pelota in Cuba: Its Evolution until 1930); Pettavino and Pye: *Sport in Cuba: The Diamond In the Rough*; and Pérez, *Essays on Cuban History*.

"There is not a city, town or district in the island of Cuba where this devouring cancer (gambling) is absent" is derived from José Antonio Saco, "La vagancia en Cuba," *The Hispanic American Historical Review* 28, no. 2 (May 1948). For the account of jai alai as a "social cancer" by Senator Manuel Sanquily, see Albert Gardner Robinson, *Cuba and the Intervention,*.

For personal accounts written by Americans fighting the Spanish-American War in Cuba, see Roosevelt, "The Rough Riders"; Richard Harding Davis, "The Battle of San Juan Hill," http://www.pbs.org/weta/reportingamericaatwar/reporters/davis/sanjuan.html). The life and times of General Leonard Wood is covered in Creelman, *Leonard Wood—The Doctor Who Became a General*; Lane, *Armed Progressive: General Leonard Wood*.

The story of First Daughter Alice Roosevelt Longworth who "shopped, ate spicy Cuban food, and followed jai alai games closely" is derived from Stacy A. Cordery, *Alice: Alice Roosevelt Longworth, from White House Princess to Washington Power Broker*. For the Cuban account of Babe Ruth in Cuba, see Méndez Muñiz, "Babe Ruth, Pelotero," *La Pelota Vasca En Cuba: Su Evolution Hasta 1930*. The story of Ernest Hemingway in Cuba is drawn from Hemingway and Brennen, *Hemingway in Cuba*.

Both the *New York Times* and the *Washington Post* in their coverage of the day highlighted the United States Senators playing jai alai: "Jai Alai in Senate: Executive Session Delves into Mystery of the Game," *The Washington Post*, March 18, 1904; "Senators Play Jai-Alai: Mimic Game on Senate Floor during Consideration of Gen. Wood's Case," *New York Times*, March 18, 1904.

Chapter 5

The history of the founding of the St. Louis Fronton is drawn from Ricardo Galbis Ajuria, "The St. Louis Fronton," Basque Studies Program Newsletter, University of Nevado Reno, November 19, 1978; Russell M. Magnaghi, "The St. Louis Fronton Revisited," Basque Studies Program Newsletter, University of Nevada Reno, November 19, 1928.

The history and culture of early Basque immigrants in the

western part of the United States follow Bieter and Bieter, *An Enduring Legacy: The Story of Basques in Idaho*; Douglass and Bilbao, *Amerikanuak: Basques in the New World*; Echeverria, *Home Away From Home: A History of Basque Boardinghouses*; Ott, *The Circle of Mountains: A Basque Shepherding Community*; Tortoricagena, *The Basques of New York: A Cosmopolitan Experience*.

"Local players used to play until their hands swelled up," the story of handball (*mano*) players in American Basque communities, is derived from Bieter and Bieter, *An Enduring Legacy: The Story of Basques in Idaho*. Through interviews and correspondence, historian David Lachiondo, whose father was a sheepherder who emigrated from the Basque Country in 1931 to Wyoming, then Idaho, says "Handball is a people's game; all you need is a wall and a ball."

The cultural history of Florida follows Allman, *Finding Florida: The True History of the Sunshine State*; Grunwald, *The Swamp: The Everglades, Florida, and the Politics of Paradise*; Hiller, *Highway A1A: Florida at the Edge*; Mormino, *Land of Sunshine, State of Dreams: A Social History of Modern Florida*.

For an overview of the history of gambling in Florida, see Klas, "Gambling's Long History in Florida"; Klas, "A Timeline of Gambling in Florida"; Thompson, *Gambling in America: An Encyclopedia of History, Issues, and Society*; "Racing and the Pari-Mutuel Industry in Florida: A Study Report" by Florida Legislature Legislative Council Committee on General Legislation, 1965; "Legalized Gambling in Florida—The Competition in the Marketplace," prepared for the Florida senate in 2004; and "Gaming: An Economic Overview," presented by the Florida Legislature in 2013.

The story of pari-mutuel jai alai in Florida follows the question of legalized gambling at the state horse- and dog-racing tracks. For "Governor Vetoes Florida Race Bill," see the *New York Times*, May 30, 1931. "It is unsound and unwise from an economic, political, or moral standpoint to commit the state to a partnership in legalized gambling in any form. If we start with the pari-mutuel, where shall we stop?" asked Governor Doyle E. Carlton, Senate Legislative Record, "Journal of the Senate," 665, State of Florida Executive Department, Tallahassee, May 29, 1931.

"Indignation is rife here among the members of the Florida winter drinking and gambling set over the veto of the Florida pari-mutuel bill and persons are going around town uttering profane remarks about Doyle Carlton, the governor of the state, and wondering how he happened to come unhitched" is derived from Westbrook Pegler, "Gov. Carlton's Race Bill Veto Shocks His Host," *Chicago Daily Tribune*, June 2, 1931.

"Without the gambling legislation, the fronton will close next year," said Miami Jai Alai's Richard I. Berenson, who fought for and achieved legalized wagering at the jai alai games. Through interviews and correspondence, Richard B. Berenson, third-generation jai alai family, relates the stories of his grandfather Richard Isadore Berenson, and his father, Louis Stanley (Buddy) Berenson.

"There are, when all's said and done, only a handful of spectator sports which make the general public's blood, and the gate receipts, flow like sap in the springtime" is taken from John Lardner, "Which Sport Has the Greatest Appeal," *New York Times*, October 24, 1954.

"The city fathers of Miami ought to erect a plaque at Northwest 36th Street and Douglas Avenue to commemorate a historic event that has influenced modern life. It might read: Exotic Race Track Wagering Was Invented Here by Richard I. Berenson" is taken from Andrew Beyer, "In South Florida, Exotic Wagering Thrives on Competition for Gamblers' Dollars," *Washington Post*, January 17, 1987.

Chapter 6

The history of the New York Hippodrome, "a palace . . . a building to rouse wonder and eagerness" is covered in Clarke, *The Mighty Hippodrome*. For the story of jai alai games played at the New York Hippodrome, see "Americans are becoming more enthused about the sport," taken from "It Takes Hold, This Jai-Alai," *New York Sun*, November 22, 1938. "We're afraid Mike Jacobs is going to have a hard time making New Yorkers act like Basques, especially on top of a heavy meal, and we're sure the Hippodrome is the wrong place to try it" is derived from Harold Ross and Wolcott Gibbs, "Debut," *The Talk of the Town*, *New Yorker*, September 17,

1938. "There's no interest in jai alai around here, Mr. Jacobs said" is derived from John Lardner, "Which Sport Has the Greatest Appeal," *New York Times*, October 24, 1954.

Miami was the "playground of the world and one of the most delightful cities in the world in which to live permanently" is taken from a 1947 promotional brochure, *Souvenir of Miami, Miami Beach, Florida*, Curt Teich & Co.

"Jai alai players were treated by segments of Miamians and visitors as celebrities," says historian Paul S. George, a native of Miami, who tells his story of jai alai in Miami through interviews and correspondence.

"Extremely good moments," says jai alai player José Ramón Eizaguirre through interviews and correspondence.

"I love the game. I started playing at twelve years old when I was a little skinny kid but was persistent and confident," says jai alai player Joey Cornblit through interviews and correspondence.

The story of allegations of corruption in Connecticut is drawn from "Tammany in Connecticut," *New York Times*, November 12, 1975; Ray Kennedy, "The Pelota Bounces Up North," *Sports Illustrated*, July 7, 1976; Steve Candy, "High Hopes for Jai Alai in Connecticut Are Soured by Scandal," *New York Times*, November 5, 1975; Robert Boyle, "The Spreading Scandal in Jai Alai," *Sports Illustrated*, June 1, 1979; "11 Indicted in Jai Alai Probe," *St. Petersburg Times*, March 1, 1980. For accounts of the statewide investigation of jai alai frontons in Florida, see Patrick Riordan and Fitz McAden, "State Giving Jai Alai the Eye," *Evening Independent*, October 16, 1979; Fitz McAden, "Politics Dictates Who Watches Frontons," *Evening Independent*, October 16, 1979.

For the story of "Jai Alai: the License to Steal," see Geraldo Rivera, ABC *20/20*, June 21, 1979; "Silvester v. American Broadcasting Companies Inc." (839 F2nd 1491), March 15, 1988, http://openjurist.org/print/344555.

Through interviews and correspondence, Bob Heussler, radio and television sportscaster based in New York City, relates his experience as director of public relations at Milford Jai Alai in Connecticut.

Chapter Seven

The story about the murder of World Jai Alai owner Roger Wheeler is drawn from Cullen and Murphy, *Whitey Bulger: America's Most Wanted Gangster and The Manhunt That Brought Him to Justice*; Lehr and O'Neill, *Black Mass: Whitey Bulger, the FBI, and a Devil's Deal*; Amy Padnani and Katherine Q. Seelye, "Whitey Bulger, The Capture of a Legend," *New York Times*, November 14, 2013. David Wheeler, son of Roger Wheeler, contributes to the background information through interviews and correspondence.

"Sometimes the sign of progress is a completely gutted building" is derived from Nick Sortal, "Dania Jai-Alai in Midst of Makeover," *Sun Sentinel*, May 4, 2015. "I want to repackage jai alai and make a unique game with great athletics better. From a business standpoint I will give jai alai my best shot to make it work," says Dania CEO Scott Savin through interviews and correspondence.

"From the first time I borrowed a cesta and threw the ball hard and it landed straight down on the floor, bounced back and hit me in the face, requiring stitches, I knew I wanted to play jai alai," says jai alai player Leon Shepard through interviews.

"I love what I do. . . . jai alai is my life's work," says jai alai player Robert Barrios through interviews and correspondence.

"I've always had a vision of making jai alai great again," says jai alai player Ben Bueno through interviews and correspondence.

Epilogue

"I was blown away when I saw my first professional jai alai," says amateur player Katie DiDomizio through interviews and correspondence. "There is something about the game of jai alai that can't be described. It instills a passion in you which does not go away," says Matt DiDomizio, jai alai player and owner of Connecticut Amateur Jai Alai through interviews and correspondence. "I grew up with jai alai" is derived from Darlene Gardner, "First Female Moving to Fronton's Center," *Sun Sentinel*, April 1, 1987.

Selected Bibliography

Abrisketa, Olatz González. *Basque Pelota: A Ritual, an Aesthetic.* Reno: Center for Basque Studies, University of Nevada Press, 2013.

Allman, T. D. *Finding Florida: The True History of the Sunshine State.* New York: Atlantic Monthly Press, 2013.

Bethell, Leslie. *Cuba: A Short History.* Cambridge, UK: Cambridge University Press, 1993.

Bieter, John, and Mark Bieter. *An Enduring Legacy: The Story of Basques in Idaho.* Reno: University of Nevada Press, 2003.

Blanchard, Kendall. *The Anthropology of Sport.* Westport, CT: Bergin & Garvey, 1995.

Blazy, E. *La Pelote Basque.* Bayonne, FR: Librairie Pialloux, 1929.

Clarke, Norman. *The Mighty Hippodrome.* South Brunswick, NJ: A. S. Barnes, 1968.

Coddon, Hal. *Jai Alai: Walls and Balls.* Las Vegas: GBC Press, 1978.

Craft, Kevin. "Will Lacrosse Ever Go Mainstream? A Look at What It Takes for a Sport to Break Through." *The Atlantic*, April 13, 2012.

Creelman, James. "Leonard Wood—The Doctor Who Became a General." *Pearson's Magazine*, volume 21, issue 4, 1909.

Cullen, Kevin, and Shelley Murphy. *Whitey Bulger: America's Most Wanted Gangster and the Manhunt That Brought Him to Justice.* New York: W. B. Norton, 2013.

Dana, Richard Henry. *To Cuba and Back: A Vacation Voyage*. Boston: J. R. Osgood, 1875.

Douglass, William A., and Jon Bilbao. *Amerikanuak: Basques in the New World*. Reno: University of Nevada Press, 1975.

Douglass, William A., and Joseba Zulaika. *Basque Culture: Anthropological Perspectives*. Reno: Center for Basque Studies, University of Nevada Press, 2007.

Dunstan, Roger. "History of Gambling in the United States." California Research Bureau: California State Library, January 1997. https://www.library.ca.gov/crb/97/03/crb97003.html.

Echeverria, Jeronima. *Home Away From Home: A History of Basque Boardinghouses*. Reno: University of Nevada Press, 1999.

Findlay, John M. *People of Chance: Gambling in American Society from Jamestown to Las Vegas*. New York: Oxford University Press, 1986.

Gallop, Rodney. *A Book of the Basques*. Reno: University of Nevada Press, 1970.

"Gaming: An Economic Overview." The Florida Legislature Office of Economic and Demographic Research 850.487.1402. January 14, 2013. http://edr.state.fl.us.

Goitia, José M., with Bob Austin. *Jai Alai: The Other Side of the Screen*. N.p., 1983.

Gray, Geoffrey. "In Basque Country, Coming Home to Jai Alai." *New York Times*, May 14, 2006.

Grunwald, Michael. *The Swamp: The Everglades, Florida, and the Politics of Paradise*. New York: Simon and Schuster, 2007.

Guttman, Allen. *From Ritual to Record: The Nature of Modern Sports*. New York: Columbia University Press, 1978.

Guttman, Allen, Joseph Anthony Mcguire, William H. Thompson, and David Charles Rowe. "Sports." *Encyclopedia Britannica Inc.*, March 10, 2017. https://www.britannica.com/topic/Sports.

Hemingway, Hilary, and Carlene Brennen. *Hemingway in Cuba*. New York: Rugged Land, 2003.

Herrington, Katherine Hines. *Jai-Alai: The First Look at America's Newest Sports Craze*. N.p.: WICC Books, 1977.

Hiller, Herbert L. *Highway A1A: Florida at the Edge*. Gainesville: University Press of Florida, 2005.

Hollander, Zander, and David Schulz. *The Jai Alai Handbook: A Bettor's Guide to the Fastest Sport in the World*. Los Angeles: Pinnacle Books.

Hosler, Dorothy, Sandra L. Burkett, and Michael J. Tarkanian. "Prehistoric Polymers: Rubber Processing in Ancient Mesoamerica." *Science, New Series* 284, no. 5422 (June 18, 1999): 1988–1991. https://www.jstor.org/stable/2898168.
Humphreys, Jeanne. *Jai Alai: Put Your Money On The Swinging Baskets*. N.p., 1977.
Klas, Mary Ellen. "A Timeline of Gambling in Florida." *Tampa Bay Times*, November 25, 2009.
———. "Gambling's Long History in Florida." *Tampa Bay Times*, November 24, 2009.
Koebel, W. H. *Modern Argentina: The El Dorado of To-Day*. London: Francis Griffiths, 1907.
Kurlansky, Mark. *The Basque History of the World: The Story of a Nation*. London: Penguin Books, 2001.
Lane, Jack C. *Armed Progressive: General Leonard Wood*. Lincoln: University of Nebraska Press, 2009.
"Legalized Gambling in Florida—the Competition in the Marketplace." Report Number 2005–155. November 2004. Prepared for the Florida Senate. Prepared by Committee on Regulated Industries.
Lehr, Dick, and Gerard O'Neill. *Black Mass: Whitey Bulger, the FBI, and a Devil's Deal*. New York: Public Affairs, 2000.
Martyr d'Anghera, Pietro, and Francis Augustus MacNutt. *De Orbe Novo: The Eight Decades of Peter Martyr d'Anghera*. New York: G. P. Putnam's Sons, 1912.
Mooney, Michael. "What Happened to Jai Alai?" *Sports Blog Nation*. February 28, 2013. http://www.sbnation.com.
Méndez Muñíz, Antonio. *La Pelota Vasca En Cuba: Su Evolucion Hasta 1930* (Pelota in Cuba: Its Evolution until 1930). Ciudad de la Habana: Editorial Cientifico-Técnica, 1990.
Mormino, Gary R. *Land of Sunshine, State of Dreams: A Social History of Modern Florida*. Gainesville: University Press of Florida, 2005.
Ott, Sandra. *The Circle of Mountains: A Basque Shepherding Community*. New York: Oxford University Press, 1981.
Perallón, José E. *Pelota Vasca*. Bilbao, ES: Edita Coinpasa, 1994.
Pérez, Louis A., Jr. *Essays on Cuban History*. Gainesville: University of Florida Press, 1995.
Pettavino, Paula J., and Geralyn Pye. *Sport in Cuba: The Diamond in the Rough*. Pittsburgh: University of Pittsburgh Press, 1994.

Roosevelt, Theodore. "The Rough Riders." *Scribner's Magazine*, vol. xxv, no. 4, April 1899.

Scarborough, Vernon, and David R. Wilcox, eds. *The Mesoamerican Ballgame*. Tucson: University of Arizona Press, 1991.

Skiena, Steven S. *Calculated Bets: Computers, Gambling, and Mathematical Modeling to Win*. New York: Cambridge University Press, 2001.

Stern, Theodore. *The Rubber Ball Games of the Americas*. Seattle: University of Washington Press, 1992.

Thompson, William Norman. *Gambling in America: An Encyclopedia of History, Issues, and Society*. Santa Barbara: ABC-CLIO, 2001.

Totoricaqüena, Gloria. *Basque Diaspora: Migration and Transnational Identity*. Reno: Center for Basque Studies, University of Nevada Press, 2005.

———. *The Basques of New York: A Cosmopolitan Experience*. Reno: Center for Basque Studies, University of Nevada Press, 2004.

Tyldesley, Joyce A. *Daughters of Isis: Women of Ancient Egypt*. London: Viking, 1994.

Urza, Carmelo. *Historia de la Polta Vasca en las Américas*. Reno: University of Nevada Press, 1994.

Whittington, E. Michael, ed. *The Sport of Life and Death: The Mesoamerican Ballgame*. New York: Thames & Hudson, 2001.

Woodworth, Paddy. *The Basque Country: A Cultural History*. Oxford: Oxford University Press, 2008.

Index

Page numbers in italic text indicate illustrations.

Abrisketa, Olatz González, 28, 50
Anduiza Fronton: Boise, Idaho, 82
Argentina: Jai Alai, 38, 54–57; changes to cesta, 18, 53
Arrasate, Juan: "Arra's Story," 16–17

Barrios, Robert, 127–28
Basque festival: jai alai, 28, 36, 62, 141
Basque homeland and identity, 22–31. *See also* Basque tradition; Euskara language
Basque pelota ball, 2, 16, 31, 34; evolution of Basque pelota games, 33–38
Basque tradition, 1–2, 10, 13–14, 22–38, 43, 53, 81–84, 124, 137, 140
Berenson, Louis Stanley (Buddy), 109, 123–24
Berenson, Richard B., 87, 109, 123
Berenson, Richard I., 87–88. *See also* Hippodrome; pari-mutuel betting
betting, 8, 12, 15–16; bad publicity, 116–17; Basque, 33–36, 105–6; betting scandal, 109, 111–14; China, 91–92; Cuba, 60–61, 67, 70, 75; spectators, 8, 15–16, 33–36, 140; United States, 78, 80–81, 84–86, 90, 93, 99, 131–32, 137
Bieter, Mark, 83

Bridgeport, CT: Jai Alai, 109, 111–14, 123–25
Bueno, Ben, 132–35
Bulger, James (Whitey), 12, 120–22

Capone, Al, 88–90
Carlton, Governor Doyle, 88–90
cesta: design and construction, 3–4, 14, 18, 21–22, 36–39, 50, 52–57, 83; throw with cesta, 14, 29–31, 69, 71, 127
cesta punta, 2, 32, 38, 62, 88. *See also* jai alai
Chicago: Jai Alai at Rainbo Gardens, 91
China: Shanghai, 103
Churruca (Francisco Maria Churruca Iriondo Azpiazu Alcorta), 51–53, 73–74, 105, 107, 131
Connecticut: Jai Alai, 112–15. *See also* Hartford, CT; Milford, CT
Cornblit, Joey, 107–9
Cuba, 8–9, 15, 59–75, 77–80, 96, 99, 108. *See also* Palace of Screams

Dania Casino: Dania Jai Alai, 53, 11–112, 126, 131–34, 139
DiDomizio, Katie, 138–39
DiDomizio, Matt, 138
Don Quixote: Miguel de Cervantes, 18

Douglass, William, 24–25

Egypt: Egypt Exploration Fund, 19; Egyptian burial sites, 19–22
Eizaguirre, José Ramón, 103–6
Etxebeste-Otegi, Joseba: "Evolution of Basque Pelota Games," 33–36
Euskara language, 22, 25–26, 33, 140

Fleischman, Marty, 9–10, 124
Florio, Hector, 2
Franco, Francisco, 26

Gabis, Ricardo, 78
Gallop, Rodney, 23, 25
game-fixing, 111–12. *See also* betting
George, Paul, 1, 101
globalization: jai alai, ix–x, 140
Goiko (Iñaki Osa Goikoetxea), 13–15, 26
Goitia, José, 10, 23, 26, 38–40, 116, 129–31
Guenetxea, Bonifacio, 26
Guinness Book of World Records: the fastest-moving ball sport, 42
Guruceaga, Melchor, 53–56, 64

handball, 2, 16, 18, 28, 31–40, 43, 57, 61–66; piece of the homeland, 82–83. *See also* Mesoamerica

Harotcha, Gantxiki, 36–37, 104
Hartford, CT: Jai Alai, 109, 111, 113–14, 123–24
Havana Fronton, 65–67, 69–70; Babe Ruth, 71–73; Churruca, 71–73. *See also* Palace of Screams
helmets, 42, 106–7
Hemingway, Ernest, 4, 71–72
Herrington, Katherine Hines, 22, 53, 103
Heussler, Bob, 43, 116–117; jai alai in Connecticut, 112–15
Hialeah Park: Fronton, 84–88, 90; racetrack, 88, 90–91, 101
Hippodrome: New York, 42, 96–99

Illoro, José Antonio, 26

jai alai: how game is played, 5–7; origin, 36–37; *partido*, 21, 104; *quiniela*, 106; traditions, 1–2, 10, 43, 82–84

"Kill Shot," 1, 8–9, 12–13, 27, 108, 142. See also *Miami Vice*
Kurlansky, Mark, 25

Lachiondo, David, 83
Louisiana Purchase Centennial Exposition, 4, 77; St. Louis Fronton, 77–80

Martirén, Gabriel: paleta, 56

Menor, Erdoza: "El Fenomeno," 21–22
Mesoamerica: ball game, 44; *pelota Mixteca*, 44–46; rubber manufacture, 43–44, 47–48
Miami Jai Alai, 15–16, 52–53, 84–87, 95–96, 99–101, 106–9, 127–31. See also *Miami Vice*; pari-mutuel betting
Miami Vice, 1–2, 8–12, 27
Milford, CT: Jai Alai, 111–16, 124–125, 138

Nevada: Basque boarding house, 81; Jai Alai, 103–4, 125, 129
Newport, Rhode Island: Jai Alai, 14, 41–43, 124, 128

organized crime, 12, 120–121. *See also* Capone, Al

paddleball, 33, 56–57
Palace of Screams, 18, 65, 70, 73, 75, 79
pari-mutuel betting, 8, 12, 88, 90–95, 101, 103, 106, 112–15, 120, 124; linked to casinos, 126, 130–31
pelota ball, 3; ball construction, 48–52; *speed of ball, 3, 9, 36, 42–43, 50, 52, 54, 73, 80, 95, 108, 127, 137 (see also Guinness Book of World* Records, 42)
pelota: Mesoamerica, 44–46;

pelota (*continued*)
  pelota a mano, 32, 62, 140; *pelota a pala*, 32; *pelota a paleta*, 56; pelota scoring, 30; pelota serve, 30–31, 67; *pelota vasca*, 9, 16, 18, 28–29, 33–34, 38, 61, 79, 81, 103, 131
pelotari, 10, 33–34, 39
players' strike, 13, 50, 57, 114, 123–24, 130, 139
play to win, *11*, 33; Etxebeste-Otegi, Joseba, 36; Goikoetxea, Iñaki Osa, 15

Roosevelt, Alice Longworth, 67
Roosevelt: First Lady Eleanor, 15; Roosevelt, Theodore, 63, 68–69
rubber ball, 9, 32, 38, 43–45, 48, 49–52, 62, 142. *See also* Mesoamerica
Ruth, Babe: Cuba, 15, 71–72

Savin, Scott: Dania Casino and jai alai, 132
Shepard, Leon, 125

Skiena, Steven, 103
Smith, Becky, 139
Stoll, Marijke Maurine, 44–46
strategy: playing jai alai, 8–9, 16, 30, 103–4, 107

Totoricagüena, Gloria, 55, 81
traditional jai alai, 1–2, 10, 43, 82–84

University of Jai Alai, 37
Urza, Carmelo, 29, 38

Wheeler, David, 122
Wheeler, Roger: *Black Mass*, 122; John Martorano, 119; murder, 12, 119–23; Whitey Bulger, 12, 120–22. *See also* Winter Hill Gang
Winter Hill Gang: Whitey Bulger, 12, 120–22
Wood, General Leonard, 65–70
World Jai Alai Inc., 9, 12–13, 109, 111, 119–22, 129

Yankee Stadium of Jai Alai, 9
Yarza, Pedro, 26